Me Be Like Jesus?

Me Be Like Jesus?

Leslie B. Flynn

While this book is designed for reading enjoyment and individual instruction, it also is intended for use as a book for group study. A leader's guide is available at 95¢ from your local bookstore or from the publisher.

Published by
VICTOR BOOKS

a division of SP Publications, Inc.
P.O. Box 1825 • Wheaton, Ill. 60187

VICTOR BOOKS
A division of SP Publications, Inc.
P.O. Box 1825 ● Wheaton, Ill. 60187

Third printing, 1974
ISBN 0-88207-234-X
Copyright © 1972, SP Publications, Inc.
World rights reserved.
Printed in the United States of America

CONTENTS

Preface **9**

Acknowledgments **11**

1. Model of Models **13**

2. So, They Insulted You **23**

3. Service With a Capital "S" **41**

4. You Aim to Please—But Whom? **51**

5. Outsiders Welcome! **63**

6. "I'll Forgive, But I Won't Forget" **83**

7. Humility of Heaven **95**

8. Jesus, the Gentleman **107**

9. In the Hour of Trial **119**

10. Joyful Jesus **131**

11. Loving Winsomeness **145**

Preface

Exactly what is Christlikeness?

One of the best known attempts to answer this question is Charles Sheldon's *In His Steps* which, except for the Bible, outsold all other books in the last century. This best-seller imagines how Jesus would act in a series of situations.

However, the kind of Christlikeness pictured in the New Testament does not spring from imaginative contemplation of Jesus' supposed deportment under certain circumstances. Rather, the New Testament singles out certain qualities in Jesus' character and bids us emulate Him in these particular temperaments.

Approximately a dozen such traits in the disposition of Christ are specifically mentioned as an example for us to follow. These virtues, explicitly spotlighted for us in the Master's conduct as a model for our own behavior, are discussed separately in the following chapters.

People today are striving after beauty of body, spending millions on the outer man. True beauty is the beauty of the soul—the culture of Christlikeness within.   LESLIE B. FLYNN

Acknowledgments

ME BE LIKE JESUS? was first published in 1962 by Zondervan Publishing House, Grand Rapids, Mich., under the title *The Power of Christlike Living.* It appears now for the first time in paper, revised and updated.

The song excerpt at the bottom of page 129 is from "When We See Christ," copyright 1941, renewal 1969 by Howard Rusthoi. Assigned to Singspiration, Inc. All rights reserved. Used by permission.

1

Model of Models

A few weeks before the Allied invasion of Nazi-held Europe across the English Channel in 1944, an English officer was assigned the unusual task of impersonating General Bernard Montgomery. To enhance his natural resemblance to the general the officer drilled in numerous details, learning to grin, salute, walk, eat, and talk like Montgomery. After several days of close personal study of the general, he mastered his role.

Whisked to Gibraltar, the new "Monty" leaked information about a special plan to invade southern France. Clever Nazi agents relayed the information to Hitler. Traveling on to Algiers and the Middle East, "Monty" let lurking informers overhear more snatches of the same secret strategy. The officer played the role so well that he not only fooled enemy intelligence but many high-ranking English brass. As a result, Hitler deployed his forces toward the south of France away from the English Channel, making it easier for Allied soldiers to get a successful foothold on the continent on D-Day.

God has a special assignment for every Christian. The ultimate aim of redemption is to make every believer resemble Jesus Christ. Only, unlike the imitation of the officer, the Christian's outward conformity is strengthened by an inward dynamic.

CHRISTLIKENESS—GOD'S PLAN

Originally God created man in His own image. Through disobedience man scarred this image. To restore this marred image God sent His Son, who was the express image of His Person. The Lord Jesus Christ lived a perfect, ideal manhood, then died on the cross to release the power to reproduce this pattern in humans. He became like us that we might be made like Him.

When a man is converted, immediately a far-reaching goal confronts him. Not optional, but predetermined, the plan calls for conformity to Christ's nature. "For whom He did foreknow, He also did predestinate to be conformed to the image of His Son, that He might be the firstborn among many brethren" (Rom. 8:29). The Bible and the church exist mainly for the cultivation of Christlikeness. The Holy Spirit's task is to make men holy after the pattern of Christ.

Though redeemed sinners do not perfectly reflect the example of Christ in this life, some day every believer will fully bear the family resemblance, likeness to the Father and the Elder Brother. The example of Christ is not only a command of what we *should* be but a promise of what we *shall* be.

CHRISTLIKENESS—GOD'S PRECEPT

Christ is both Saviour and Example. The church hasn't always maintained relationship between these two truths. At times stress has been laid on imitation of the Master to the neglect or denial of the atonement. On the other hand, emphasis on pardon and peace through the blood of the cross has on occasion almost crowded out accent on conformity to the character of Christ. Those who omit salvation through the blood nullify the Gospel, while those who fail to underscore the believer's responsibility to follow the model of Christ emasculate the truth.

To be sure, Christ is needed as Redeemer before He is to be imitated as Ideal. A man told a preacher after a sermon on the death of Christ, "I'd rather hear a talk on the example of Jesus!"

"Would you be willing to follow Him if I preach Christ as an example?" asked the minister.

When the man agreed, the preacher replied, "Let us take the first step." Then he explained, "After the Bible says that we should follow Christ's steps, it states in the next verse about Christ, 'Who did no sin.' Can you take this step?"

The man looked confused. "No, I do sin and readily admit it."

"Well, then," said the preacher, "your first need of Christ is not as an example, but as a Saviour from your sins!"

Many try to walk in the steps of the Master who haven't taken the first step, which is to receive Him as personal Saviour. After that we follow Him.

Both the Lord and the apostles clearly declare that Christ came to be not only Saviour but supreme Model for human behavior. For instance, after washing His disciples' feet the Lord said, "I have given you an *example*, that ye should do as I have done to you" (John 13:15).

So indelible an impression was made on sword-swinging Peter by the Lord's non-retaliatory reaction in His final hours, that he wrote, "If, when ye do well, and suffer for it, ye take it patiently, this is acceptable with God. For even hereunto were ye called: because Christ also suffered for us, leaving us an *example*, that ye should follow his steps" (1 Peter 2:20, 21).

In approximately a dozen areas the New Testament specifically points to the example of Christ as a pattern for us to follow. We need to look clearly and meditatively at each of these traits of the divine portrait. Not only will this exercise give a distinct impression of what God wants us to be, but by beholding the glory of the Lord, we may actually be changed into the same image.

John Owen, 17th century Vice-Chancellor of Oxford University, wrote, "If our future blessedness shall consist in being where He is and beholding His glory, what better preparation can there be for it than a constant previous contemplation of that glory as revealed in the Gospel, that by a view of it we may be gradually transformed into the same glory?"

CHRISTLIKENESS—GOD'S PORTRAIT

Exactly what is Christlikeness?

It is not physical resemblance to Christ. Physically the Lord looked like other men. On the night of the betrayal Judas had to arrange a sign so those arresting Jesus would know which one was He.

Nor is it a cultural similarity. If it were, then, if some descriptions of first-century Holy Land customs can be trusted, we would walk about in sandals, wear long-flowing robes, speak Aramaic, and men would have beards. Independent of culture, Christlikeness transcends the customs of time and place.

Nor is it following Him in every outward step and circumstance. If we imitated Him literally, we would be carpenters till age 30, then leave our secular work for three years of itinerant teaching, avoid marriage and family life, show little interest in art, science, or national affairs, often sleep outdoors, and go about penniless. Many medieval Christians mistakenly thought that to fully follow Jesus they had to take vows of celibacy and poverty.

Many think that Christlikeness is imagining what Jesus would do in every situation, then following His supposed course of action. Such contemplation can be provocative. However, a major difficulty is that our conclusions are based on *imagining* what Jesus would do. Often our answer becomes the mere projection of our wishes or opinions. Some people think Jesus would attend a good movie; others are convinced He would not even watch television. Some folks suppose Jesus would drink socially in moderation; others are just as sure He would be a total abstainer. The kind of Christlikeness the New Testament enjoins does not spring from fallible speculation on Jesus' hypothetical behavior under certain conditions.

Christlikeness is having the mind of Christ, to catch His spirit, to cultivate His qualities, to apply these attitudes to every situation. It goes without saying that where Scripture is plain, such as in the clear-cut application of the Ten Commandments, the mind of Christ need not be sought, for it is already enunciated. But since detailed rules of universal moral application have not been spelled out in the Bible to cover every individual case, the mind of Christ will have to be our guide. Often, the motive behind an act is much more important than the overt deed itself. Long prayers offered by Pharisees seem outwardly commendable, but when covering up an embezzlement of widows' property or parading religiosity, such petitions turn out to be sheer hypocrisy. The quality of a deed in isolation is much less significant than the quality of mind from which it springs.

Thus we are to follow Christ in certain inward qualities, temperaments of spirit, frames of mind. This explanation of Christlikeness may prove disappointing to those who like cut and dried rules. But if our inward disposition can become like Christ's, our outward behavior will reflect His likeness.

These qualities involved in Christlikeness, because timeless and changeless, belong to no particular age and culture but adapt to every period, place, or situation. Even though Christ never married, His example can lift marriage to its highest level. In fact, the strongest command given to husbands refers to Christ's example. "Husbands, love your wives, even as Christ also loved the church, and gave Himself for it" (Eph. 5:25).

Significantly, Christlikeness resides not in the realm of doctrine, as necessary as orthodoxy may be, but in the area of disposition. It is possible to contend for a correct creed with a contentious, un-Christlike bitterness. Both are needed—right belief and Christlike spirit.

Here are the qualities of Christlikeness specifically singled out in the New Testament for our emulation:

non-retaliation	(1 Peter 2:21-23)
menial serving	(John 13:14, 15; Matt. 20:28)
humility	(Phil. 2:3-8)
gentleness	(2 Cor. 10:1)
self-denial	(Rom. 15:1-3; Matt. 16:24)
patient under trial	(Heb. 12:1, 2; 1 Peter 3:17, 18)
forgiving	(Col. 3:13)
friendly to outsiders	(Rom. 15:7)
joyful	(John 15:11; 17:13)
obedient	(1 John 2:6; 3:2, 3; John 15: 9-12)
loving	(Eph. 5:2, 25; John 13:34; 16: 12; 1 John 3:16)

How like the varieties of the fruit of the Spirit are the qualities of Christlikeness. "The fruit of the Spirit is love (loving), joy (joyful), peace, long-suffering (forgiving, non-retaliation), gentleness, goodness (menial service), faith (faithfulness, obedience), meekness (patience under trial), temperance (self-denial)."

Similarity between Christlikeness and the fruit of the Spirit is not surprising, for the work of the Holy Spirit is to produce the holy character of Christ within the believer.

CHRISTLIKENESS—GOD'S PROVISION

Christlikeness involves much more than mere outward imitation. To emulate the pattern of Christ in the outer life takes the power of Christ in the inner life. James Stalker who wrote an excellent treatise on *The Image of Christ* pointed out three defects in the otherwise excellent medieval classic on the same theme, *Imitation of Christ,* by Thomas a Kempis. He said the latter work is suited for residence in a monastery, not life in the outside world. Also, it fails to stress the need of forgiveness as a basis for imitation. Finally, it doesn't emphasize internal union with Christ as a source of exterior imitation.

Christlikeness is not laboriously achieved by effort and vigorous self-discipline. Christlikeness unfolds from within, as we obey the indwelling Christ. It is the inevitable expression of His unfolding life. For a non-Christian to live the Christian life is impossible. Mahatma Ghandi asked for an impossibility when he said, "I wish I could be Christlike without being a Christian."

The example of Christ by itself does not suffice. If the dramas of Shakespeare, or the paintings of Rembrandt, or the compositions of Beethoven were placed before you as examples from which you were to create similar masterpieces, you would fail because you lacked the inward genius of these men. The example of Christ's matchless life cannot be reproduced unless an inward impulse is imparted.

A son often resembles his father in looks, tones, gestures, walk—almost laughably so. Why is this likeness so accurate? Partly because of his continuous opportunity to observe his father and thus unconsciously imitate. More than this, the boy at birth received his father's nature, so that something within is responsible as well as the father's example without. To live Christ we must be able to say with Paul, "Christ liveth in me."

The outliving of this Christ life is not automatic. The New Testament knows nothing of the workings of the Spirit of Christ in us apart from our own moral responses in faith and surrender. Watchfulness, prayer, conscious effort and intelligent cooperation in the program of God are requisites to progress in Christlikeness. Also, the New Testament demands a conscious and determined approximation to the example of Christ. To cultivate this resemblance to Christ's frame of mind, outlook, aims, spirit, qualities, attitudes, and disposition, we are specifically commanded to observe the matchless portrait of Christ. But all this eager striving will be but useless beating of the air unless we have received inner grace.

Andrew Murray put it thus in *Like Christ*, "If

Jesus Himself through His life union will work in me the life likeness, then my duty becomes plain, but glorious. I have, on the one side, to gaze on His example so as to know and follow it. On the other, to abide in Him, and open my heart to see the blessed workings of His life in me."

The Holy Spirit uses Christ before us to help reflect Christ within us.

The winsomeness of Christlikeness provides a powerful method of drawing people to the Christian faith. A wealthy family was scheduled to entertain a famous minister who was coming for a series of services in their town. The mistress sent the maid downtown to buy the finest cut of meat, adding, "I want the best for the minister."

In the butcher shop the maid sneered, "Some saint is coming to our town to speak, and my mistress is entertaining him. I must have the finest cut of meat. You would think that the Lord Himself is coming."

A few days later the maid returned to the butcher shop for more meat. She seemed subdued and quiet. The butcher asked how she was getting along with the saintly visitor.

Meekly the maid replied, "A few days ago I said you would think that the Lord Himself was coming. I want you to know I think I have seen the Lord this week!"

Do others see the Lord in you?

2

So, They Insulted You

Back in the days of slavery a plantation own-
er who suffered financial reverse was forced to sell
Cuff, who had served him faithfully. His new master was an atheist. "You'll find Cuff a good worker
in every way except for one thing," he told the
atheist.

"What's that?"

"He'll pray quite a bit, and you can't break
him of the habit. But that's his only fault."

"I'll soon whip that out of him," threatened the
new master.

"I wouldn't advise you to try, for Cuff would
rather die than give up," were the former master's
parting words.

Cuff was faithful to his new master, obeying
orders, sweating from morning to night. But he
prayed. Word reached the master. Angrily he sent
for him. "Cuff, you must not pray anymore. Never
let me hear any more such nonsense."

Cuff replied that he loved Jesus and had to pray, and that, besides, praying made him love his master better and, work harder.

"I don't care; we don't want it here. If you pray again, you'll be taken out and flogged," the master threatened.

Despite the order, Cuff prayed. The master heard of it and summoned him. "Why have you disobeyed me?"

Cuff replied that he had to pray; that he could not live without it.

The master flew into a temper, ordered Cuff tied to the whipping post, and cracked the whip over his raw back five times. Then he kept on bringing the lash on the bleeding back. Cuff's wife ran out. He threatened to beat her. Finally out of exhaustion he stopped beating the slave, ordering salt rubbed into his wounds. Ordered back to work, Cuff went away singing.

Cuff worked faithfully the rest of the day. That night the master couldn't sleep. He was convicted of his cruelty. He woke his wife and asked if she thought anyone on the plantation would pray with him. She suggested Cuff.

"Do you think he would pray for me?" he asked.

"Yes, I think he would," his wife replied.

Cuff was summoned. When the messenger found Cuff, he was praying, and thought sure he was in for another beating. Brought into the master's presence he was amazed to hear him ask, "Oh, Cuff, can you pray for me?"

"I've been prayin' for you all night!" Cuff replied. He spoke of the Saviour to the master, who became a believer. Both of them toured the nearby vicinity telling the Gospel.

By his patient behavior Cuff obeyed Peter's command to slaves to follow the example of Christ. "For even hereunto were ye called: because Christ also suffered for us, leaving us an example, that ye should follow His steps, who did no sin, neither was guile found in His mouth, who, when He was reviled, reviled not again; when He suffered, He threatened not; but committed Himself to Him that judgeth righteously" (1 Peter 2:21-23).

Our Lord's actions in connection with His crucifixion encourage a meek nonretaliation in the face of abuse and invective. In fact, we are specifically told that Christ's long-suffering without complaint or counterblast is a model for us to follow.

The word "example" alludes to a schoolboy's copy-slate on which the writing-master wrote characters which were to be copied carefully. Likewise, penned for us in Sacred Writ are the indelible strokes that spell out the Saviour's silent suffering in the face of rankest, rudest mistreatment, which we are commanded to studiously imitate. With the words "follow His step," the figure changes from copy-slate to a path along which we are urged to follow Him who went this way before us.

The sufferings of Christ were unique in regard to the atonement, for none of us can suffer as the Saviour and thus provide forgiveness for others. Yet the sufferings of Christ with respect to reaction to scurrilous maltreatment provide a pattern for similar conduct by those who profess to be His followers.

HE REVILED NOT

The vendetta, in which obligation rests on relatives of a murdered or wounded man to take blood vengeance on the person who has caused death or injury, still prevails in some quarters. But the Lord Jesus Christ never undertook a vendetta against those who conspired against His life or the life of His friends.

When growing up He learned of Herod the Great's attempt on His life which forced His family to flee to Egypt and which caused the slaughter of innocent babes, but He instituted no revenge against the descendants of wicked Herod. Nor did He seek vengeance on another Herod who beheaded His cousin, John the Baptist.

After preaching in His hometown of Nazareth, He was rejected by His own neighbors, who tried to throw Him over a precipice. His reaction was, "A prophet is without honor in his own house." Though He marveled at their unbelief, He did not revile them.

The people in Jairus' house laughed Him to scorn when He suggested Jairus' daughter was not dead. He didn't return the mockery by shouting, "I'll show you!" but restored her to her parents. He never sulked or nursed resentment.

The blasphemous accusation of being in league with the devil was hurled at Him by the Pharisees who said that He cast out demons by the prince of demons. The Lord didn't castigate them in reply, though He did show them the absurdity of their charge.

When ordered out of an area after healing demon-possessed men, He didn't say, "I'll go, but first let me tell you something," then proceed to give His hearers a piece of His mind, and later report, "I sure gave them an earful!"

To be called insane is not easy to take. Jesus' brothers made light of Him, suggesting He was out of His mind (Mark 3:21). No retaliatory remark escaped His lips.

When the Pharisees took counsel to slay Him He didn't call down twelve legions of angels but quietly withdrew from the area (Mark 3:6, 7). To the officers sent by the Pharisees to apprehend Him, He spoke gently and graciously so that the soldiers returned to the chief priests empty-handed saying, "Never man spake like this man" (John 7:32-46). Repeatedly His enemies sought to arrest Him, but no man laid hands on Him, because His hour was not yet come. Neither is there a record of a nasty word hurled by our Lord at His would-be murderers (John 7:30; 8:20, 59; 10:31, 39).

Invectives against our Lord during His ministry were sporadic and scattered. During the final 24 hours of His life insults became concentrated and almost continuous. When the yelling mob came to arrest Him in the garden, He simply asked, "Whom seek ye?" When He told them, "I am He," they toppled backward to the ground through the majesty of His person, not through any retaliatory blow by Jesus. Had He wished, He could have discharged thousands of angels to wipe out this band of Romans. He didn't revile Judas, who was then committing one of the vilest acts of treachery in human history. Rather He allowed Judas to kiss Him and even called the traitor, "Friend" (Matt. 26:50). When Peter drew his sword and cut off the ear of one opponent, Jesus restored the ear.

Soviet Premier Khrushchev on a visit to a French Cathedral said, "There is much in Christ that is in common with us Communists, but I cannot agree with Him when He says when you are hit on the right cheek, turn the left cheek. I believe in another principle. If I am hit on the left cheek I hit back on the right cheek so hard that the head might fall off." How different from Christ! Few persons have ever been reviled like Jesus Christ. No one has reacted so magnificently. And we have been commanded to follow suit.

False witnesses accused Jesus before Caiaphas and the Sanhedrin, but He was silent. "He held His peace" (Mark 14:61). He did not fume back. Then the chief priests, scribes, and elders mocked Him, buffeted Him, blindfolded Him, and slapped Him, sneering "Prophesy, who is it that smote Thee?" Many other blasphemies they threw in His face (Luke 22:63-65).

Accused before Pilate by the chief priests and elders, He answered nothing, which made the governor marvel. Sent to Herod because He came under His jurisdiction, Jesus was mocked by Herod, set at nought or made a zero, and dressed up in a gorgeous make-believe royal robe (Luke 23:9-11). He took it sweetly.

Pilate ordered Jesus scourged. The cruel whip lashed His back, cutting deep and even swishing around to gash His front. The soldiers scoffingly placed a crown of thorns on His brow, outfitted Him in a kingly garment, put a reed in His hand as a make-believe scepter, bowed as if to worship, and saluted the "King of the Jews" (Matt. 27:27-31). Then they spat on His face, and, with the spit dripping down His face and hanging from His beard, they wrenched the reed from His hand, smote Him on the head, pulled off the robe and put His own raiment on. He never struck back by word or deed.

Historians report that when a man was about to be crucified he would invariably struggle against his executors as they tried to hold his arms so a nail could be hammered through his hand. The victim would squirm, scratch, kick, bite, scream, swear, spit at his tormentors until he had been securely hung up. Not so with Jesus. Instead of hurling vile vituperation he prayed, "Father, forgive them; for they know not what they do" (Luke 23:34).

Lifted up for all to see, He became an object of sarcasm. Passersby wagged their heads, "You said You could rebuild the temple in three days. Save Yourself, if You are the Son of God. Come down from the cross." The rulers, chief priests, scribes, and elders derided Him, "He saved others; Himself He cannot save. Come down from the cross and we will believe you." The soldiers jeered; both thieves at first cast the same scoffings in His face. "If Thou be the Christ, save Thyself and us." But all through the six hours of the cross, not a cry of revenge broke the stillness. Seven short sayings, uttered at an average of one an hour, revealed the anguish of His soul, words only of redemption, not retaliation. How humiliating for the Lord of glory to take such abuse from sinful, loathsome creatures. But Thomas a Kempis in his book, *Of the Imitation of Christ*, says, "He deserves not the name of patient who is only willing to suffer as much as he thinks proper, and from whom he pleases. The truly patient man asks not from whom he suffers, his superior, his equal, or his inferior; whether from a good and holy man, or one who is perverse and unworthy. But from whomsoever, how much soever, or how often soever wrong is done him, he accepts it all as from the hand of God, and counts it gain."

To stand on our rights, claim our privileges, return evil for evil and blow for blow, to demand our pound of flesh does not reflect the Lord Jesus Christ who gave His back to the smiters and His cheek to those that plucked off His hair, who hid not His face from shame and spitting (Isa. 50:6), and who, as a sheep before her shearers is dumb, opened not His mouth (Isa. 53:7).

The cross of Christ stands not only as an act of unique atonement, but also as an example of patience under sufferings. In the hour of mistreatment our Lord does not expect us to perform an act of redemption for sin, for this has been effected once-for-all by Christ's vicarious death, but He does require that we follow in His steps and bear the injustice without recrimination. Admittedly, this precept becomes complicated when interwoven with other duties such as the protection of others

against violence, but when it involves only ourselves in a personal situation, the injunction remains clear.

HE RESTED IN DIVINE JUSTICE

The silence of Jesus in the face of injustice
was not due to any failure on His part to recognize
as evil the abusive treatment He was suffering. But
His calm behavior evidenced deep faith in the
moral government of the universe. Though evil
wore a crown while good was nailed to a cross, He
believed that His Father reigned on the throne and
someday would make all things right, punishing
wrong and rewarding right.

Hence He told His disciples that if they were
rudely received in a city they should shake off the
dust from their feet as a symbol of future judgment when it would be more tolerable for Sodom
than for that city. But judgment on that city was
the Lord's business, not theirs. "Vengeance is
Mine, saith the Lord." Should a person speak vilely
to us, he puts himself in danger of judgment (Matt.
5:22); but should we revile him in return, we likewise make ourselves candidates for judgment. Far
better to commit the insult to the Judge above and
thus follow the steps of Christ.

Nonreviling doesn't necessarily mean a person
should not answer back. Before the Sanhedrin
Jesus was asked if He were the Christ. He didn't
keep silent at this point but affirmed that He was
the Messiah, adding that they would "see the Son
of man sitting on the right hand of power, and

coming in the clouds of heaven" (Mark 14:62).

When an answer was needed to vindicate the truth, Jesus answered. When an answer was pointless, no reply was forthcoming. When reviling was in progress, an answer would only add fuel to the fire. But to the tempting Satan He replied, "It is written." He defended His association with publicans and sinners. He upheld the practice of cornpicking and healing on the Sabbath. He did not hesitate to correct error, "Ye have heard that it was said, but I say unto you. . . ." He defended Mary's use of expensive ointment against the claim of waste. When the Pharisees charged Him with casting out demons by the devil, His reply made their accusation misfire. When criticized because His followers transgressed the tradition of the elders, He retorted by charging His accusers with violating the commandments of God. To the Pharisees who claimed He was bearing false record of Himself, He answered kindly but firmly. In fact, many discourses in John's Gospel are replies to unbelief and false charges. When the Pharisees and Sadducees tried to trap Him with trick questions, He answered, and answered so well He left them gasping. So, nonretaliation doesn't rule out defense.

Nor does a nonreviling attitude forbid rebuking. He rebuked His disciples for their little faith and hardness of heart. He reproved Martha for overagitation on mundane matters. He scolded Peter, "Get thee behind Me, Satan: thou art an offence unto Me: for thou savorest not the things that be of God, but those that be of men" (Matt.

16:23). He warned against the doctrine of the Pharisees. He called them to their faces "an evil and adulterous generation" (Matt. 12:39). He rebuked but never reviled.

He even became angry at times, in righteous indignation pronouncing woes on the hypocritical Pharisees, castigating the money changers in the temple. Jesus' scathing scorn was never the result of personal vindictiveness but stemmed from love of righteous principles. A magazine article asked, "Do You Act—or React?" Too often we let other people's remarks and actions determine what our responses will be. It would be better for us to so possess the life of Christ within, that snubs, criticisms, and harsh accusations would not disturb our inner serenity. Intemperate reaction indicates that we are controlled by the situation, rather than in control.

So often in our heated remarks we are egged on by pride and self-defense. When an object is thrust near our face our eyes close in self-defense. When an object moves in our direction, we automatically raise a hand to ward off the blow. Likewise a sense of proud honor jumps to defend us against any slight or insult of our person, egging us on to return evil for evil. Christ's anger was objective, impersonal, without malice. So much of ours is subjective, personal, and spiteful. Many arguments around the home would never occur if we yielded to Christ's power within and His pattern without.

The Son cared not for His own honor, only the Father's honor, which He defended by reply, rebuke, and sometimes righteous wrath. The Son knew that the Father would care for the Son's honor ultimately, and thus entrusted all revilings to the Father who someday will judge righteously.

A preacher confided in a friend, "I'm going to resign. I've been mistreated by members of my church!"

The other asked, "Have they crowned you with thorns yet? Or did they spit on you? Have they nailed you to a tree?"

The preacher saw the point and continued his pastorate.

HE RETURNED GOOD FOR EVIL

Not only did our Lord refrain from reviling when reviled, but more than that, He returned good for evil and blessing for cursing. At His arrest He restored the ear of the high priest's servant. At the crucifixion He did not rail at His tormentors but instead prayed, "Father, forgive them, for they know not what they do." To the repentant thief who had previously joined his voice in mocking Him, Jesus promised, "This day shalt thou be with Me in paradise." The first two of the seven cries from the cross were words of blessing in return for reviling. Even while being blasphemed, He was in the process of earning redemption for those calling Him names.

This kind of conduct astounded His viewers. Governor Pilate earlier had marveled at His silence (Matt. 27:14). The centurion in charge of the crucifixion was moved by such behavior to exclaim, "Truly this was the Son of God" (Matt. 27:54). Fifty days later 3,000 people changed their minds about Him, calling Him their Saviour and Lord, many of whom, if not the majority, probably insulted Him during His sufferings. To remain silent under provocation is so unnatural that it helps people to believe in the supernatural. When the first martyr, Stephen, was being stoned to death, he never picked up a single stone to throw back. Instead, following Jesus' example he prayed, "Lay not this sin to their charge" (Acts 7:60). Not long after this a young man who guarded the clothes of those who stoned Stephen, and who was the leading opponent of the early Christians, capitulated to Christ on the Damascus road. One of the pricks that goaded Saul of Tarsus toward Christ was the memory of Stephen's deportment.

Vituperation, insulting abuse, and invectives will not persuade the non-Christian to trust in Christ. A woman went to her pastor to request him to speak to her husband about becoming a Christian. The pastor did and was told that the wife had a hot temper. "If this is what Christianity does to a person, I want nothing of it," the husband replied. The pastor relayed the husband's complaint to the wife. She was shocked but realized that the charge was true. She fell before the Lord in penitent prayer. The next week when the husband entered the living room after a fishing trip, his protruding pole accidentally knocked over his wife's prize lamp. Crash! The husband put his hands over his ears to drown out the next expected crash—his wife's scorching rebuke. But after a momentary silence, he heard her say, "Don't worry about that lamp, dear. What's a lamp? We can always replace it!" He could scarcely believe her reaction. A few weeks later he made a profession of faith in Christ, whose beauty had been seen in his wife's life as she followed His example.

When two prize chickens wandered into a neighbor's vegetable patch, the neighbor wrung their necks and tossed them over the fence whence they had come. The woman next door, seeing her chickens fly over her fence and land with a thump on her lawn, ran out to the still flapping birds. Her children wondered what their mother's reaction would be: angry denunciation of the ill-tempered neighbor, tears, or crying on father's shoulder when he came home. To their amazement she proceeded to make two delicious chicken pies, one of which she took to the neighbor with an apology for the damage her chickens had done to the vegetable patch. The children hid behind a bush to see the neighbor's expression. He who never lacked words to express his anger stood speechless and ashamed.

A soft answer not only stops anger, but stirs up amazement. Turning the other cheek, walking the two-mile way, helping those who hate us, and praying for our persecutors, are among the most potent ways of advertising the Gospel. Thereby Christ is seen in all His majestic strength of character.

A Spanish evangelist in Latin America was eating dinner in a restaurant before the evening service. Fastidious about his appearance, he was impeccably dressed in a white linen suit. Suddenly the waiter slipped and spilled soup on the evangelist's coat and trousers. With profuse apologies he cringed before the evangelist, for waiters had been known to lose their jobs through such carelessness. But the evangelist, who was slightly burned, jumped to his feet and quickly reassured the waiter and the manager that all was well, even though he knew it meant preaching in soiled clothing. The next night the evangelist returned to the same restaurant. About to leave he saw the waiter beckon. He followed him to a side room, where the waiter begged him to tell how he could have acted so kindly instead of letting loose with a string of oaths. The evangelist told him of Christ, who when reviled, reviled not again.

To behave like that requires the power of Christ within. Only then can we follow the pattern of Christ without. A nurse complained to a preacher that she had been rudely treated by some of the patients. "Thank God," replied the preacher.

"What do you mean?"

"Why," said the minister, "if you are carrying a dish and someone bumps you, you can only spill out of the dish what's inside. Since you have Christ within, Christ will spill over." To trace in daily life the model of Christ in Holy Writ we need the might of Christ in our heart.

When Walter "Happy Mac" MacDonald, well-known evangelist of years past, became a Christian in 1925 in the Pacific Garden Mission on State Street in Chicago, the old crony who ridiculed him the loudest was "Doc." Though he never learned Doc's last name, MacDonald had made his acquaintance while he was in big-time vaudeville in Chicago and Doc was a barker for a dive where, standing out on the sidewalk, he would chant with a big, gravel voice, "You're just in time for the next show." MacDonald used to take several barkers into speakeasies during Prohibition and treat them to a drink. Doc, a big-boned, middle-aged six-footer with heavily lined face, hated the Pacific Garden Mission which was just a few doors from his dive. The other barkers hated it, too, for many a star performer was lost to these joints through finding Christ in the mission.

"It's unhealthy for our business to have that mission right in the same block," Doc would often say. But MacDonald didn't have the same dislike for the mission, and unknown to his friends he had been attending meetings there for weeks. He always made sure his friends never saw him go or come, for he wanted to save face with them.

But came the night when MacDonald was transformed by Christ. The hard-drinking, fast-dancing, big-time comedian discovered real joy. Thrilled to know the reality of sins forgiven, he wondered what his old pals would say when they found out. He avoided them for a week, but, knowing he had to face them sooner or later, he started down State Street one night. An old pal spotted him, "You louse! We ain't got no use for you! Beat it!"

Nearing Doc's place he heard his voice ring out, "The geereatest and biggest show in all Chicago!" He broke off, "Well, if it ain't little Reverend Happy Mac. Happy, say it's a lie. Say it ain't true that them mission heads got my old pal."

"No, Doc, it isn't a lie. I've become a Christian. I'm through with the old life. I'm even helping out in services leading singing."

Doc wanted no more of it. He warned, "I might bring some of the boys and drop in on you at the service some night!"

Sure enough, next night, Doc and another barker stood outside while Mac led the singing, all the time flapping their arms and mimicking him. Says Mac, "The fact I didn't lose my temper but kept on singing was proof I had new life."

The climax came when eight friends met MacDonald on the street one night, lined up, four on each side. As he walked between them and spoke, they chanted, "One, two, three, ptoo!" They spit on his new tan suit and shoes. Unlike his old self, Mac responded, "Your aim is excellent, Doc. Caught my new trouser leg and my shoe."

Doc growled back, "That all you got to say?"

"Not quite, Doc. There's this. When you get to know Jesus Christ the way I do, you'll be able to unclench your fists. You'll let a guy spit on you, and it'll be all right!"

MacDonald didn't see Doc for three weeks until one night he showed up in the mission, on the front row. As the invitation was given, MacDonald slipped beside him. "You're not mad at me, Mac?" Doc asked.

"The Lord won't let me get mad anymore."

"Mac, you been a Christian long enough to know how to lead a guy to Jesus?"

"Yes, Doc."

"Then, I'm your customer." That night Doc accepted Christ. Then he showed Mac a letter that had been the reason for his coming to the mission. His mother was dying and he was preparing to go to her bedside. He had promised her years before he would become a Christian but had never come within miles of keeping his word.

Two weeks later Doc was back in Chicago. He had spent just three hours with his mother before she passed away, overjoyed at her son's decision. Doc still continued as a barker on the street, only this time inviting people into the Pacific Garden Mission. One day two weeks later he dropped dead on the sidewalk. Says MacDonald, "I thank God from the bottom of my heart for the day old Doc spit on my tan shoes and trousers."

An old Spanish proverb says, "To return evil for good is devilish; to return good for good is human; to return good for evil is godlike." We would make a slight change, "To return good for evil is Christlike."

3

Service With a Capital "S"

Famed opera singer Jerome Hines walked unheralded into the Union Gospel Mission in Chattanooga, Tenn., one evening to sing for society's unfortunates. Fresh from successful appearances at the Metropolitan Opera in New York and the famed La Scala in Milan, Italy, he had come to the city for a concert in Memorial Auditorium. He sang hymns and testified that for years he had stumbled around as a spiritual panhandler till the Lord found him. When several men responded to the invitation, the physically imposing six-foot, seven-inch singer, who commands thousands of dollars for concert appearances, left the platform to kneel beside a man to pray with him.

In stooping to lowly service, this giant singer is following the example of Him who, though greater than all, condescended to menial tasks. The Creator and Sustainer of the universe became not only man but servant, tending the needs of His creatures. He gave us a pattern of humble ministry which He commanded us to follow. He taught that true greatness doesn't consist in attaining first place to be served by others, but in willingness to drop to an obscure spot to serve even a little child for the sake of Christ (Mark 9:34-37).

Often the disciples argued among themselves who would be chief in the coming kingdom. Once their ambition-laden dispute incongruously followed the Lord's disclosure of His coming death. Another time James and John aspired through their mother's intervention to the two top seats in the kingdom. The Lord answered that heathen men sought to land number one positions so as to wield power. But Christ's followers were to be the opposite. "Whosoever will be great among you, shall be your minister; and whosoever of you will be the chiefest, shall be servant of all." Then to offset the lofty attitude of His disciples He introduced the example of His own lowly service, adding, "For even the Son of man came not to be ministered unto, but to minister, and to give His life a ransom for many" (Mark 10:43-45).

Most graphic of all occasions when the disciples fought over future leadership was when the Lord not only taught lowly service but followed with a memorable demonstration.

During the Paschal supper, with the Saviour's cross less than 24 hours away, the reclining disciples inappropriately fought among themselves who should rank the highest. Again our Lord patiently admonished them.

Then He asked, "Whether is greater, he that

sitteth at meat, or he that serveth? is not he that sitteth at meat?"

The fillip came when the Lord declared that He was the waiter: "I am among you as he that serveth" (Luke 22:26, 27).

At this point, according to some scholars, Jesus rose from His place to do a servant's chore. Common courtesy demanded that a host should at the arrival of guests wash their feet soiled by treading dusty streets. Because the upper room was borrowed, no person was present to take care of the usual ablutions. But basin and towel had been thoughtfully provided. Who would do the honors? With the atmosphere charged with feverish ambition, no aspiring leader would abdicate his throne of ambition to kneel before his subjects. Looking away from the towel and basin with studied indifference, each regarded this task too menial for his dignity.

Then something amazing happened. Jesus rose from His place and picked up the basin and towel. The Lord of Glory—at whose beckon legions of angels were ready to serve with instantaneous response—with full consciousness of His divine glory, chose the servant's place, taking the soiled feet in His own hands.

When He had gone the rounds, He stated in language which must have fallen with thunderlike intensity that they were to follow His model.

"If I then, your Lord and Master, have washed your feet; ye also ought to wash one another's feet. For I have given you an example, that ye should do as I have done to you" (John 13:14, 15).

Though a majority of believers do not believe the Lord meant that we should establish a foot-washing ordinance, none of us can escape the clear injunction to serve others in need, including those on a lower social scale.

Late one night during a conference at Moody Bible Institute, D. L. Moody was walking around the halls to see that all was in order. Turning a corner, he came upon the guest rooms where some visiting English preachers were sleeping. Outside each door was a pair of shoes.

Moody remembered the European practice which called for placing one's shoes outside the door on retiring so the host could polish them before morning.

Spotting several students, he said, "These ministers are following the custom of their country where they always put their shoes out to be cleaned at night. Would you fellows get a piece of chalk from a classroom, put the number of the room on the soles of the shoes, then shine them nicely."

One student protested, "Mr. Moody, I didn't come to this institution to clean shoes. I came here to study for the ministry." The others said the same.

"Very well," said Moody, "you may go back to your rooms."

Then Moody himself collected the shoes, took them to his room, polished them nicely, and put them back in place.

An interesting sidelight in the career of the distinguished apologist and seminary professor Dr. J. Gresham Machen occurred during World War 1. Applying for service with the overseas YMCA, he was first assigned the lowly task of manufacturing and selling hot chocolate drink in quarters in a French village. The involved process consisted in shaving up large bars of sweet chocolate, adding a fixed quantity of boiled water, then adding a larger quantity of water, all the time mixing the chocolate in, bringing the whole to a boil, adding condensed milk and then ending with a final boiling. To open the canteen at 7 A.M. meant rising much earlier to prepare the hot drink and postponing his own breakfast till after 9 A.M. Though he wished for heavier responsibility, especially in Christian service, this ordained and scholarly professor was content with the opportunity to perform such menial service.

Meanness of work never lowers a person. Rather, the spiritual law of rank says the higher you wish to stand the lower you must stoop to serve.

The Lord served in various ways, such as teaching, preaching, and healing. He it was who broke the bread and distributed it to His disciples. He it was who replenished the refreshments at the wedding at Cana. He arranged for the Upper Room, broke the bread and distributed the wine at the Last Supper. The Lord of Glory served!

In the Emmaus home after the resurrection, He who was guest became host and again He broke bread. On the seashore in the third post-resurrection appearance to all the disciples He prepared the fire, had fish and bread laid thereon, then used the fish the disciples caught, issuing the invitation, "Come and dine." Apparently, He was the cook.

Peter described Him as one "who went about doing good, and healing all that were oppressed of the devil" (Acts 10:38). All the time He was Master He was also Servant, answering the call for help and ministering to the needy.

How brimful of activity our Lord's days must have been! In his *Harmony of the Gospels* A. T. Robertson terms the events recorded in Mark 3:19—5:21 a "busy day," just one of many such in the Master's ministry. In the morning He teaches a crowded audience. He is insulted. Later His mother and brothers try to take Him away as mentally deranged. In the afternoon He relates an unusual group of parables, some of which He privately interprets in a home. Toward night He crosses the lake by boat, so tired that he sleeps soundly amid the howling storm. On the other side He heals the Gadarene demoniacs, then returns the same night. What a toilsome day!

The supreme service He performed was the giving of Himself in redemption. This work is listed as a separate ministry. He came to minister "and to give His life a ransom for many." Even while giving His life on the cross, He ministered to the spiritual cry of the dying thief and took care of His mother.

So strongly does the example of Christ's service dominate early Christian thinking that the titles given leaders in the Early Church signify service. A minister is simply one who ministers or serves—a servant. The word *deacon* comes from a verb which means to *minister* or *serve*. A pastor is a servant-shepherd of the flock. A bishop is an overseeing servant. Church leaders are not bosses but servants, as are all Christians.

Though heaven cannot be earned by works, the concept of service stands prominent in the Gospels and epistles, not only in spiritual tasks like witnessing and giving, but in physical ministrations. Some positive applications of the law of service include relieving illness and pain, helping the mentally distressed, affording hospitality to strangers, visiting the aged, comforting the sorrowing, befriending the outcasts, and feeding the hungry.

During World War 2 the vice-president of a bank on Wall Street found himself weighed down with extra work imposed by the war. Yet he took time four nights each week, after a hard day's work in the city and a weary commuter's ride to his New Jersey community, to act as volunteer orderly in the nearby veterans' hospital. He fed, washed, and readied for bed warshocked soldiers.

Pure religion involves not only separation from worldliness but visitation of the fatherless and widows in their affliction (James 1:27).

Even the insignificant favor of a cup of cold water in Jesus' name will not go unrewarded—and even when offered to a despised person or child.

The parable of the Good Samaritan teaches that service must be extended to anyone in need that crosses our path, regardless of color or creed.

Americans live in a land blessed beyond measure materially. With 6% of the world's population, America consumes one-half of the world's resources, spends one-half of all the money, eats one-seventh of all the food, uses one-half of all the bathtubs, has 10 times more doctors than the other 90%, and enjoys a per capita income of $4,000 as against a per capita average of $200 for the rest of the world. Have American Christians no responsibility to these unfortunate multitudes who are so in need?

The Lord taught that in the day of judgment sheep will be separated from goats. The division will be based on the performance or neglect of simple ministrations. Those on the King's right hand will hear Him say, "Come, ye blessed of My Father, . . . for I was an hungred, and ye gave Me meat: I was thirsty and ye gave Me drink: I was a stranger, and ye took Me in: naked, and ye clothed Me: I was sick, and ye visited Me: I was in prison, and ye came unto Me" (Matt. 25:34-36).

Does this contradict the Gospel of grace which says salvation comes through faith and not by works? No, but faith without works is dead. If we have genuinely experienced the mercy of Christ through faith, then we cannot help but express that faith through our actions. Failure to do good to the less fortunate may indicate that we have not truly experienced the mercy of Christ.

Significantly, our Lord told the disciples to wash each other's feet because He had done the same to them (John 13:15). Because Christ stooped in lowliness to us, we should stoop to lowly deeds for others. Consciousness of personal relationship to Christ motivates kindness in our dealings with others. He served me, so I should serve. If I serve not, perhaps I've not been served by Christ.

The Pharisees bound heavy burdens on men's shoulders, but would not lift a finger to help them. How unlike Christ, the great Burden-bearer! Lack of sensitivity to the loads of others indicated they had never been relieved of their load of sin.

A man was praying with great fervor in a prayer meeting for a family whose husband and father had suddenly died. "O God, do send someone to bring comfort to that sorrowing family. . . ." Suddenly his voice faded. Quietly he left the meeting. Before the service closed, he returned.

Asked why he had so abruptly finished his prayer and left, he replied, "As I asked God to touch that grief-stricken family, He seemed to tell me that I was to go and touch them for Him."

Our whole duty to our fellowman was summarized by our Lord as "love to neighbor" (Matt. 22:39). This duty Paul restates in this fashion, "By love serve one another" (Gal. 5:13, 14).

When Sir Bartle Frere, great English philanthropist and one time governor of Cape Colony, wrote his wife in London that he was coming home, she called the new coachman. "I want you to go to the station to meet your master," she told him.

He politely bowed. "But your ladyship, I have never seen Sir Bartle. How shall I recognize him at the station?"

She thought for a moment, then proudly replied, "Look for a great big man helping somebody. That will be my husband."

At the station cabs and carriages crowded the area. The coachman looked up and down the platform and saw a great many big men. Then he saw a woman who was trying to get out one of the train doors, but she was wedged in with a big box and suitcase. Suddenly a tall man, morning-coated, came and raised his silk hat politely.

"Madam, may I help you?" Relieving her of all her bundles he asked, "Where are you going?"

She said, "I wish a cab, sir."

He took her across the platform, hailed a cab, then put her in, giving the cabbie directions.

As the cab drove off the coachman stood there. He saluted, "Is this Sir Bartle Frere, sir?"

"Why, yes, who are you?"

"I am your coachman, sir."

"Oh, yes, I remember. My wife told me the other man had left. And so you are my new coachman."

He was about to climb into the coach when he stopped. "By the way, how did you know me?"

"Please, sir, her ladyship said I was to look for a big man helping somebody."

This isn't a bad definition of Christlikeness. Someone helping someone else because he has first been helped by the greatest of all Helpers. Sir Bartle Frere delighted to carry other people's burdens because Jesus had carried his.

Our sense of debt to Christ should urge us to faithful, unpretentious service. Out of gratitude for His grace that redeemed us from our guilt, we should gladly minister to those in distress. With the pattern of Christ without, and with the power of Christ within, we should go about doing good, as He did. Even at best, we shall still be unprofitable servants.

4
You Aim to Please—
But Whom?

A married couple with no children was asked by the transportation committee of a church if they would pick up two brothers from a disinterested family and bring them to Sunday School each week.

As the only church members living in that area, the couple thought over the assignment. It would mean rising earlier every Sunday, driving several blocks out of their way, perhaps getting the car dirty from wet feet on rainy mornings. And it might hamper their frequent Sunday pleasure trips. They said no to the transportation committee.

But this is not the scriptural way. Christians are told not to please self but to please others."

This command is reinforced by reference to Christ's example. "For even Christ pleased not Himself; but, as it is written, The reproaches of them that reproached thee fell on Me" (Rom. 15:1-3).

We do no irreverence to our Lord to assume

that He would have found it much more pleasant to remain where He could enjoy the privileges of heaven than to suffer the privations of earth. Had He selfishly pleased Himself we would not know the joys of redemption.

He temporarily abdicated His residence, reputation, riches, rest, even life itself. These comforts He voluntarily surrendered that we might enjoy the glories of salvation. Christlikeness demands denial of self for the benefit of others.

RESIDENCE

The Lord gave up His heavenly home to come to earth. To a would-be follower, Jesus pointed out that though the birds had nests and the foxes had dens, He had no place to pillow His head (Matt. 8:19, 20).

At the end of a busy teaching day in the temple His hearers retired to the relaxation of their homes. But Jesus kept walking through the streets of Jerusalem, passed through the gate and climbed the mount of Olives, doubtless His frequent sanctuary for sleep and prayer. "And every man went unto his own house. Jesus went unto the mount of Olives" (John 7:53; 8:1).

In His final hours He said, "In My Father's house are many mansions" (John 14:2). No one knew better than He the mansions He had left behind.

In leaving His heavenly residence Christ left the immediate, intimate fellowship of His Father in glory, though He communed with Him in cease-

less prayer. With full consistency He could say to
a potential disciple who wanted to take care of
a dying father, "Follow Me; and let the dead bury
their dead" (Matt. 8:22). Or, "He that loveth father
or mother more than Me is not worthy of Me"
(Matt. 10:37).

When Jesus asked James and John to move
out from under their father Zebedee's roof, He had
already practiced what He preached, for He had
left His Father's residence.

Christlikeness demands willingness to relin-
quish family ties despite the anguish it may cause.
Self-indulgent church members little realize the
torn hearts of missionaries as they leave their young
children at schools on the field for months at a time,
or at school in the homeland not to see them for
five years.

About to return to their field in Argentina, one
couple wrote, "As sailing date approaches, we know
the Lord will continue to be sufficient as we leave
our son and daughter behind at school, and say
what may well be our final good-byes to our aged
parents until we meet on eternity's shores."

Are you willing to deny yourself your TV to
attend Sunday evening service? Or the warmth of
your fireplace to join the prayer meeting? Or the
comfort of an easy chair to go out on visitation for
the church?

RICHES

A well-educated skeptic was trying to tell a
humble believer that the Bible nowhere stated that

Jesus Christ had any existence before He came into the world. They were standing on a train platform. The believer said he was sure the Scriptures were full of verses on the preexistence of Christ but wasn't making much progress in the argument. Then an informed preacher appeared. Both men turned to him, "What do you think about the question?"

"One verse settles that for me," he said.

"What verse?" asked the skeptic.

"It is 2 Corinthians 8:9, 'For ye know the grace of our Lord Jesus Christ, that, though He was rich, yet for your sakes He became poor, that ye through His poverty might be rich.'"

"Well," retorted the skeptic, "how does that prove the question?"

"Tell me," replied the preacher, "when was He rich? Was He rich when He was born in a stable and cradled in a manger? Was He rich when He worked at the carpenter's bench in Nazareth? Was He rich when He had to say, 'The foxes have holes and the birds of the air have nests, but the Son of Man hath not where to lay His head'?"

The humble believer's face lit up. "I know when He was rich."

The preacher's train pulled in at that moment. As he stepped on board, he heard the believer pressing the question to the skeptic, "Tell me, tell me, when was He rich?"

The preincarnate Christ possessed inestimable wealth. Though He owned the cattle on a thousand hills, He subjected Himself to poverty. As an incentive to some early believers to give generously, Paul introduced the example of Christ. "Though

He was rich, yet for your sakes He became poor, that ye through His poverty might be rich." Because Christ denied Himself riches which were rightfully His, we should give sacrificially.

That Joseph and Mary lacked earthly goods is revealed in the offering they brought to the temple at the dedication of the baby Jesus. The proper offering was a lamb and a pigeon or dove (Lev. 12:6). But the poor were permitted to bring a second dove or pigeon instead of the costly lamb (Lev. 12:8). Joseph and Mary offered the alternative sacrifice (Luke 2:24).

When the Lord began His public ministry, He depended partly on the financial support of women (Luke 8:2, 3). The disciples pooled what little money they had in a common bag with Judas as treasurer. When the disciples plucked corn on the Sabbath, it was because they were hungry. The practice of picking standing corn was permitted the wayfaring and the hungry, part of a Jewish program for the poor.

When the Herodians subtly asked Jesus if tax money should be paid Caesar, the Lord asked for a penny. He probably had none.

When tax collectors asked Peter for his Master's tax, the Lord provided the tax money by having Peter hook a fish in whose mouth Peter found a coin.

For many important events of His final week He had not the wherewithal. He used someone else's donkey for the so-called triumphal entry. When the disciples asked where they should prepare the passover, He gave directions to a borrowed room. Most people make provisions for their final resting-place by purchasing a plot in advance. He was laid away in someone else's sepulcher. At His death He had no possessions except those on His back, His clothing, which was divided before His eyes as He was dying.

Such an example gives sharp emphasis to His warnings against covetousness. It also explains why early believers sold their property to help their needy brothers.

Christlikeness does not require believers to take a vow of poverty. But it does demand self-denial in the midst of crass materialism.

How little sacrifice is known today! One Sunday School class decided that at Christmas they would not accept gifts from their teacher, but would together, students and teacher alike, bring an offering for an Alaskan orphanage.

A couple about to spend a lavish sum on a nonessential item pondered Christ's refusal to indulge self and gave the money to their church's missionary fund.

What if every professing follower of the rich One who became poor began immediately by denying himself the purchase of some prospective luxury, and instead gave the money to the less fortunate?

REST

Some men in public life cannot step out on the street without recognition and the crowd's adulation. Hence they eat their meals in hotel rooms, travel with bodyguards, use private elevators, and keep their whereabouts secret. Yet from the beginning days of His public ministry, the Lord's fame catapulted Him into the limelight, which robbed Him of His privacy. Crowds thronged Him, bombarding Him with requests for service.

When four men brought a palsied fellow for healing, the crowd so blocked the door that they had to let the patient down through the roof (Mark 2:4). Jesus once ordered a boat readied lest the mob crush Him (Mark 3:9). So great was the pushing multitude on some occasions that He and the disciples could not eat (Mark 3:20; 6:31). Another time the crowd was so large He had to preach from a boat (Mark 4:1). One day He was so tired that He fell asleep in the back part of a boat in the midst of a storm so violent that seasoned sailors despaired of safety as wind and waves almost submerged them.

No political campaigner ever hit the road harder than Christ, nor endured greater rigors.

He often rose early to find a solitary place to pray (Mark 1:35). He prayed all night before choosing the Twelve (Luke 6:12). Would you deny yourself sleep to show up at an early morning prayer session?

When the Samaritan woman neared Jesus, who was sitting down because He was weary, He could have rationalized, "I'm too tired to talk to her." But He didn't please self. Despite weariness He proceeded to lead her to trust in Him.

How willing are we today to answer a call for service which may mean getting dressed up, leaving a favorite pastime or book, taking time and energy to go somewhere out of the way? Jesus repeatedly surrendered whatever plans He may have had to meet the problems of others.

A Sunday School teacher was invited to a picnic on Saturday afternoon. Though his family went, he felt he should make some visits. While he frankly wished he were sitting in a nice cool spot under the shade of an apple tree, he ploddingly made his calls. One was at the home of a little boy recently brought to Sunday School by a neighbor. Though the mother did not let him in, she later invited him back. As a result both parents were eventually won to Christ.

Had Jesus remained in heaven His peaceful existence would not have been interrupted. But He chose to give up the tranquility of glory for the turbulence of earth. To be like Him calls for relinquishment of rest, ease, and comforts to help others who are restless, uneasy, and in discomfort.

RIGHTS

Though the incarnate Christ did not abandon His deity on coming to earth, He did forego some of the rights of deity. Though He was the omnipresent One, He became subject to the limits of space. Though omnipotent, He learned like other children.

Christians are sometimes called on to surrender, for a while, certain rights to help weak Christians grow stronger. In the church at Rome some weak believers had scruples against eating meat and against nonobservance of Sabbaths. Strong Christians, like Paul, knew that eating meat did not defile nor was it necessary to observe days. But to keep overscrupulous believers from stumbling, Paul suggested a surrender of rightful liberties (Rom. 14:21). He sums up his argument thus, "We then that are strong ought to bear the infirmities of the weak, and not to please ourselves. Let every one of us please his neighbor for his good to edification." At this point he supports his argument by the example of Christ, who "pleased not Himself" (Rom. 15:1-3).

Insistence on our Christian freedoms may sometimes bring disaster to weaker saints. Had Christ insisted on His, no church would exist today. One man said, "Since Christ gave up His rights, I willingly deny myself the liberty of imbibing strong drink lest my influence drag others into the whirlpool of alcoholism."

LIFE

Not only did Christ give up for us His residence, reputation, riches, rest, rights, but even His very life. Paradoxically, He who was the author of life and called Himself the *Life* permitted Himself to be cut off out of the land of the living. No man took His life but He laid it down of Himself (John 10:18). He parted from life that we might partake of it.

Most believers can quote the well-known John 3:16 about God so loving the world that He gave His only begotten Son. But few can quote the other John 3:16, specifically known as 1 John 3:16, "Hereby perceive we the love of God, because He laid down His life for us: *and we ought to lay down our lives for the brethren.*"

Christlikeness may call for the supreme sacrifice of dying for others. Jim Elliot, one of the five young men martyred by the Auca Indians, wrote, "We have bargained with Him who bore a cross, whose emphasis was upon sacrifice. Let nothing turn us from the truth that God has determined that we become strong under fire, after the pattern of the Son." He also wrote, "He is no fool who gives what he cannot keep to gain what he cannot lose."

The non-Christian attitude seeks to please self at the expense of others, whereas self-denying love seeks to please others at the expense of self. Both priest and Levite failed to inconvenience self in any way as they passed by their wounded countryman. But the Good Samaritan put self-pleasure aside, interrupted his travel schedule, expended time, energy, and money to help the unfortunate Jew.

A prisoner at Rome, Paul wrote the Philippians that only Timothy had a genuine interest in them. Not one of Paul's other helpers was sufficiently selfless to make the trip to Philippi. They were too occupied with the promotion of their own affairs. Their love of ease, family, and comfort made them unwilling to sacrifice their own quiet security. This indicated to Paul that they hadn't yet learned very deeply the self-denying service of Christ (Phil. 2:20, 21).

An official of a church was asked why he hadn't supported a week of special meetings in his church.

He replied that he couldn't shut down his business even one night in the week an hour earlier. But the following month he shut down his business, not just an hour earlier, but closed up entirely for a whole week to take a hunting trip.

A pastor called on a young man several times to persuade him to teach some teen-age boys in Sunday School. After many refusals his wife exclaimed, "Why don't you tell the preacher why you're refusing?"

He confessed it was because he played golf through the week and on Saturday morning, some of which he would have to give up for lesson preparation and teaching. The pastor pressed the challenge. The young man cut down on his golf and took the class. A few months later he walked down the church aisle during an evangelistic campaign with the sixth and last boy to become converted in a class of 13.

Later the pastor asked, "Has cutting down on golf been worthwhile?"

Tears flooded the young man's eyes as he jubilantly replied. "This is the greatest day of my life. Now I'd far rather spend my time telling others about Christ. I'm only sorry I didn't begin to teach years ago instead of wasting my time on less important things."

Self-renunciation is the essence of following Christ. Jesus gave of Himself. Do you yield to the Spirit of Christ within so that like Christ you can say, "Thy will, not mine, be done in my life! Thy pleasure, not mine!"?

5

Outsiders Welcome!

In the book *In His Steps* author Charles M. Sheldon movingly portrays how Virginia, a young lady from the upper register of society, takes an outcast, alcoholic girl into her fashionable home to live, against the wishes of her horrified, aristocratic grandmother.

Driving in a carriage with several members of her smart set through the slum section of their city, Virginia is startled when the door of a notorious saloon suddenly opens and out reels a young woman. When the girl leers up at the carriage rolling by, Virginia recognizes her as the one she had prayed with after an evangelistic meeting a few nights previously. Virginia, who recently had taken the pledge to live as Jesus would live, had felt it her duty to sing the Gospel in some services in the slums, though she lived in a mansion on the boulevard and her voice often graced the concert stage.

"Stop," cries Virginia to the driver. In a flash

Virginia leaps to the drunken girl's side, puts her arm around her, and calls her by name, "Loreen!" The girls in the carriage are smitten with astonishment. "Drive on," Virginia calls, "I'm going to see my friend home." The girls in the carriage gasp at the word "friend."

The carriage moves on and Virginia is alone with Loreen, except for some derelicts from the slums who look on with little expression. "Where does she live?" When no one answers, it dawns on Virginia that this wreck of humanity has no home. Then the thought flashes across her mind, "What's to hinder me from taking Loreen home? Why shouldn't this homeless wretch, reeking with the smell of liquor, dirty and ragged, be cared for in my own home instead of being assigned to strangers in some hospital or place of charity? What would Jesus do?" Her decision made, she takes Loreen by the arm and steers her toward the trolley stop at the corner.

Virginia painfully notes the stare of passengers on the crowded trolley. But her concern now centers on the approaching scene with her wealthy grandmother.

As they leave the streetcar and walk up the avenue with its lovely mansions, Loreen lurches heavily against Virginia time and time again, which makes people curiously turn and gaze at them. When they mount the steps of her handsome house, Virginia breathes a sigh of relief even in the face of the interview with Grandmother Page.

As Loreen stares blankly at the magnificent furniture, Virginia says to her grandmother, who has entered the hallway, "I have brought one of my friends home. She's in trouble, has no home, and I'm going to take care of her here for a while."

Gulping in amazement, Grandmother Page asks, "Did you say she is one of your friends?"

"Yes," Virginia affirms in a clear voice, recalling a verse in the Bible which speaks of Jesus as a friend of sinners.

With a cold, cutting, sneering tone, the grandmother replies, "Do you know what this girl is?"

"I know she is an outcast. She is drunk at this minute. But I saw her kneel at the altar in the services the other night and ask to be forgiven. And I also see the devil reaching out to lure her back into her old life. By the grace of Christ I feel the least I can do is to give her a home for a little while to help keep her from slipping back. So I have brought her here and I shall keep her. After all, this house belongs to me!"

Madam Page clenches her fists, glares at Virginia, and says, "We'll lose standing in society. This is so contrary to our social code. How can you be familiar with the scum of the streets?" Virginia puts her arm more tightly around Loreen. The grandmother stamps her foot and threatens emphatically, "I shall not stay in this house!" In a few hours she packs and leaves.

Whether she knew it or not, Virginia was obeying Paul's command, "Receive ye one another, as Christ also received us" (Rom. 15:7). Also, she was following the example of Christ, who in His dealings on earth with teeming humanity welcomed outcasts, outsiders, and outlaws. If the

exalted Lord Jesus Christ received us in our unlovely status, should we not likewise welcome the
unacceptable?

> Did you ever stop to think
> How lonely God would be
> If the only folks He loved
> Were those as good as He?

During His ministry He rubbed shoulders with
rich rulers and poor widows. He accepted invitations to dinner at the home of the self-righteous
Pharisee Simon and the penitent publican Matthew.
He fellowshiped with adults and took babies
and children in His arms. Multitudes moved Him
to compassion and He had time for interviews with
the individual. A large share of His energies were
devoted to the sick, while He still showed concern
for the healthy. He paid attention to both white-
collared lawyers and menial fishermen. His wide
scope of influence was foreshadowed in His infancy
when poor shepherds and rich Magi came to adore
Him.

Human nature often fawns before the ruler, the
rich, the righteous, the mature, the robust, and the
respectable, at the same time slighting those on
a lower social rung. Though receiving both types,
the Lord never hesitated to rebuke the so-called
higher levels. While a guest in a Pharisee's home,
He permitted a woman known to be a sinner in
the city to anoint His feet, and chided His host
for self-righteousness. He warned of the leaven of
the Pharisees and Sadducees, pronouncing a seven-
fold woe on the religious leaders, even calling
them, "Hypocrites, wicked and blind leaders of the

blind." His failure to scrape before celebrities earned Him the reputation of fairness. His opponents said to Him, "Neither acceptest Thou the person of any" (Luke 20:21). Literally, "You do not receive the face." Our Saviour was not a face-receiver, looking on the outer status and welcoming people because they were important or rich. He was not guilty of discrimination or snobbery. Let us follow Him in His welcome for the socially stigmatized, the Samaritans, and the sinners.

1. Women

Though not exactly stigmatized, women and children were considered inferior to men on the social scale. They are still treated as mere chattel in some countries. Before World War 2 a Westerner noted an eastern man riding on an animal while his wife walked several feet behind. After World War 2 he asked the native if the war had made any difference in the treatment of women. "Oh, yes," he replied, "I still ride on the animal, but my wife walks several feet in front of me." When pressed for a reason he explained, "That's in case there are any land mines that haven't exploded!"

From the beginning Jesus welcomed feminine followers, including Mary, Martha, Mary Magdalene, Joanna, Salome, and Susanna, who not only listened to His teachings but ministered to His material needs. Even women ostracized by society were recognized by Him. Women followed Him on His last journey from Galilee to Jerusalem, aided Him on the way to the cross, watched His burial, prepared spices for His interment, were first at the tomb on the resurrection morn, and were the first to announce His rising from the dead. Certainly womanhood was lifted to a status before unknown in the history of their sex by the Lord's attitude toward them.

2. Children

In some areas missionaries must not say anything nice about a child. Some pagans believe that the gods are jealous of children. So as not to excite their jealousy they call their children by terrible names. Should a missionary admiringly exclaim, "What a lovely baby," the mother would be frightened lest the gods in jealousy snatch this little life from her. Unlike these envious gods, the Lord Jesus Christ lifted childhood to a new level of honor by His loving actions and words. When His disciples tried to keep mothers from bringing their babies to Him, thinking these infants in arms a nuisance to Him, Jesus sternly rebuked the disciples and said in effect, "Allow the babies to come to Me. They're no bother. Don't stop them, for of such is the kingdom of heaven." Then He took the infants in His arms and offered a blessing.

He upgraded childhood by putting a child on stage and pointing to it as an example of humility. Childlikeness, not childishness, is a requisite for entrance into God's family.

We tend to disparage child conversions. "Oh, it's just a child responding to the invitation to accept Christ," someone slightingly remarks. D. L. Moody once reported that he had had two and a half conversions the night before. "You mean—two adults and one child?" "No," said Moody, "two children and one adult. The adult only has half a life to live."

3. The Sick

Some healthy people find sick people a burden and do not wish to be bothered with them. A little boy who limped found himself left out of sports by playmates who didn't want to adapt their games in any way to his handicap. A blind woman found few people who would read to her or take her for a drive. Some persons feel squeamishly self-conscious if seen in the presence of the disfigured or deformed.

Not so with Jesus. He received all the sick brought to Him. Descending from a mount, He met a leper. Others were repulsed by the sight of a man full of leprosy and hurried away. Today some people close their eyes or even become nauseated when they view missionary movies that vividly picture ulcerous sores of lepers. But Jesus touched them! Once He healed 10 lepers, men who were forced to cry "unclean" and live outside the towns and villages.

A blind man sat at a table at a Bible conference. Some Christians studiously avoided that table. In addition to the inconvenience of guiding his hand to his fork, knife, and spoon, was the gnawing embarrassment of sitting in the company of a blind person. But Jesus received many blind people. He took one man by the hand, led him along the road to the edge of town, and healed him (Mark 8:22-26). More than once He put His fingers on what may well have been most "unsightly" eyes. When blind Bartimaeus persisted in calling out to Jesus as He walked along the highway, Jesus didn't pretend not to hear but welcomed him. If we are like Jesus, supernatural receptiveness will overcome natural repulsiveness.

Some people mock the blind and make fun of the deaf and dumb. A little girl suffered a speech impediment. Another girl who attended Sunday School and should have known better kept asking her questions just to hear her stammer and make other children laugh at her. Jesus received a man who was both deaf and impeded in speech, and healed him (Mark 7:32-37).

The demon-possessed presented unlovely sights. Two wild, fierce men, naked, living outdoors in the wilderness, able to break off any chains put on to bind them, were visited by Jesus, who cast out the demons. Though demon-possession may not be prevalent in our culture, many are mentally retarded or emotionally ill. A harmless, mentally retarded boy, big for his age, was rejected by other children and mistreated by other parents who continually hollered at him, "Get off our porch. Go away from here." Paul says we should receive one another, even as Christ received us.

After World War 2 a radio announcement near Christmas urged relatives of veterans hospitalized with mental illness to visit them during the holiday season. It stated that one-quarter of 50,000 mental inmates had not received a visit from a relative for a year or longer.

Many state hospitals have patients who have been pronounced well and who could leave the institutions immediately if only there were homes to receive them.

Our Lord received all types of sick people. Seeing the multitudes He was moved with compassion on them, healing their diseases (Matt. 14:14). He welcomed the lame, the dumb, the tormented, the man with the withered hand, the palsied, the fevered, the impotent man who had been an invalid for 38 years, the woman with an issue of blood 12 years, the woman bowed and bent for 18 years, the epileptic.

A few miles north of New York City, Camp Joy, operated by the Rev. Mr. Win Ruelke of the Children's Bible Fellowship, runs several weeks of camping for mentally retarded and handicapped children. The loving reception given these afflicted boys and girls reflects the welcome Jesus always gave the sick.

4. The Poor

A young woman who dedicated her life to live as the Lord Jesus would have her live was walking up the main street of her city one morning. Just in front of her she noticed a woman carrying two big black bundles. Tagging along were two untidy little children. The woman was a foreigner who had just come in from the east on the morning express. Her clothes were mussed and her head was covered by a dirty handkerchief. The Christian girl says, "I felt a strong impression to speak to her and offer help, but with it came a feeling of repulsion. What would people on the street think? They might take her for my mother and these filthy children for my sisters. I tried to get rid of the thought that it would be like Jesus to help her, but just as I was passing her, she turned and asked if I could give her directions to the bus terminal. I was going right by there myself, so now couldn't doubt that God wanted me to help her. What a struggle for a moment, but His grace enabled me to reply, 'Yes, I'm going right there and will show you the way. Let me take one of those bundles for you.' I took the bundle for Jesus' sake, though I felt as if a fire raged at the roots of my hair. It seemed everyone was staring at me and laughing. To make things worse, one of the children began to bawl loudly. Then I was sure everyone was looking at us. But I marched on for Jesus' sake, even taking the other bundle so the mother could carry the weary baby. When I put the bundles on the seat in the bus station waiting room, I had to turn aside and weep, for the blessing of God came on my soul." She knew the joy of Jesus in receiving the poor and needy.

The poor had a large place in the Saviour's heart. When John the Baptist asked proof of Jesus' Messiahship, Jesus replied, "Tell him that the poor have the Gospel preached to them."

5. The laboring class

In some circles, perhaps unwittingly, people give greater honor to the white-collared, professional man than to the fellow who works in overalls. Yet, for His first four disciples, our Lord called fishermen, not executives sitting behind glass-topped desks. None of us has anything to say about our birth, but our preexistent Lord consented to be born in a carpenter's home, of a peasant maiden of low estate, in a run-of-the-mill family. He became a carpenter at the bench, working with tools. No wonder He invited to come to Him, "All ye that labor and are heavy laden" (Matt. 11:28), those toiling and bearing difficult burdens.

He received the commoners of this world. A young woman who moved in society circles had a maid help her now and again. She made the domestic eat all her meals by herself, even when only the family was eating. Quite often she shared the maid with her mother, who was a Christian. Whenever the maid ate at the mother's she was invited to eat with the rest of the family as an equal. The Lord received many who were considered last down here but who in divine judgment may well someday be considered first.

6. Those with some record of shame

The dying thief was pardoned by the Lord. A man with a prison record, he found a welcome from the Saviour. One class of persons in modern society who sometimes have a strike or two against them are ex-convicts trying to go straight. It may well be that too harsh treatment has been dealt those who have run afoul of the law and paid their debt. A young man who had been in jail secured a job he liked very much as night clerk in a downtown hotel. After three weeks of faithful work, he was spotted at his desk one night by a detective.

The detective then told the manager that he had an ex-convict working for him. The manager fired the man. The ex-convict later got into more trouble and ended up behind bars.

Our Lord spoke of visiting those in prison as well as the stranger, sick, ill-clad, and hungry. His welcome extends to all outcasts, including the brokenhearted and the bruised, and all who are socially "different." At a summer Bible conference a speaker approached the snack shop after the evening service. It was his custom to eat with the other speakers and distinguished conference leaders. As he entered the dining room he spotted an odd-looking fellow sitting alone at a table, while most other tables were filled with conversation and gaiety. The hostess mentioned that this fellow had asked for company. The speaker went to that table and spent the next half-hour in conversation with this lonely Christian man who had driven 100 miles to attend the conference over the weekend. Would not Christ have done this? If Christ were to welcome us as we receive others, perhaps He would have to leave us out.

WELCOME FOR THE SAMARITANS

The Samaritans were outsiders, second-class citizens, in the mind of the Jews of Jesus' day. But our Lord welcomed the Samaritans equally with His own people. Early in the Gospel record we read, "And He must needs go through Samaria" (John 4:4). The Jews usually deliberately avoided Samaria on their trips from Galilee to

Jerusalem. On that trip Jesus joined in conversation with a Samaritan woman.

His lack of prejudice constantly asserted itself. When asked for a definition of a neighbor, He replied with a story commonly called the parable of the Good Samaritan, which tells how a Jew, who was seriously beaten by thieves and deliberately bypassed by a Jewish Levite and priest, was mercifully doctored and provided for by a Samaritan. Our neighbor is anyone in need regardless of race, national origin, or creed.

An optometrist had just set up his office in his home in a new neighborhood in Los Angeles, when his first customer walked in to have her glasses fixed. After examining them the optometrist said he could find nothing wrong. The patient confessed, "I know they're all right. It was just an excuse to come in and get acquainted and make you feel welcome." This experience made the optometrist's heart glow, for his was the only Japanese-American family in the neighborhood.

During Christ's ministry the Jews were the chosen people. The Samaritans and the Gentiles were the outsiders. By His welcome of these outside groups Christ stood against anti-Gentilism. Today the tables are reversed. The church is composed chiefly of Gentiles; the Jews are the outsiders. The example of Christ's welcome to all is given to urge Gentiles and Jews to receive each other in the church at Rome (Rom. 15:7). Some of the converted Jews wishing to join the church at Rome still held to Sabbath-keeping and kosher meats. Paul urges the Gentiles to receive these on confession of faith (Rom. 14:1). The group without scruples and the group with scruples should not judge or condemn each other but live the Christian life in good conscience before God. Paul exhorts both groups, "Receive ye one another, as Christ also received us."

No Christian should be guilty of anti-Semitism. If Christ received those beyond the pale of Judaism, we should welcome those beyond the borders of Gentilism. Anti-Semitism which once expressed itself in the extermination of six million Jews by Nazi Germany in a systematic, scientific, businesslike way, is unnatural, inhuman, and irrational.

Some Americans speak disparagingly or think condescendingly of immigrants from other countries. Perhaps our prejudices take in more groups than we realize. During World War 2, a woman phoned a USO Committee. "I'll be glad to have three soldiers for dinner next Sunday at 1 o'clock," she said. Then she added, "I don't want Jews." Her doorbell rang at 1 o'clock sharp on Sunday. Answering the door she found three black soldiers standing there. One spoke up, "I understand, lady, that you want three soldiers for dinner today." Taken by surprise she replied that some mistake had been made. The soldier smiled, "I don't think Sergeant Cohen made a mistake."

Someone has said that "the most segregated hour of the week is still 11 o'clock Sunday morning." Though people tend to gravitate in their social and church life along nationalistic and ethnic lines, is it Christlike to shut the door and exclude anyone because of his nationality or color, especially after the Sunday School has taught the boys and girls to sing, "Red and yellow, black and white; They are precious in His sight; Jesus loves the little children of the world"? Since 1952 all of Billy Graham's crusades have been integrated. Though campaigns have been held in every part of the South, sometimes with one-third of the audience blacks, practically no unpleasant incidents have occurred.

The story is told of a Sunday morning service in a fashionable church in Richmond, Virginia, shortly after the Civil War. When communion was being served, a black man who had entered the service walked down the aisle and knelt at the altar. Resentment rustled through the congregation. Suddenly a distinguished layman stood up, stepped forward, and knelt beside the black. Captured by his magnanimous action, the entire congregation followed suit. The layman was Robert E. Lee.

WELCOME FOR THE SINNERS

A major problem of Brazil is public prostitution. In a small Brazilian town some girls involved in this immoral practice came to the Presbyterian mission hospital for treatment. After giving them medical care, a fine Christian doctor witnessed to them of the Gospel of Christ, then invited them to the local church. A few weeks later half a dozen of them hesitantly walked into the morning service and sat timidly by themselves. At the end, when nobody spoke to them, they left hurriedly. They returned the next Sunday. Soon there was an uproar.

The righteous women of the congregation were up in arms. They didn't want those women to dare to come in the church. Word indirectly reached the girls; they never came back.

Christ's pattern would show the attitude of the church ladies to be un-Christlike. When on earth, the Lord accepted the woman of Samaria who had had five previous husbands and was at that time living with a man who was not her husband. Rather than withdraw from this stained soul, He led her to believe on Himself as the Water of Life so that she became a flaming witness to her own neighbors who knew her unsavory reputation well. Jesus said on one occasion to the religious but self-righteous leaders, "That the publicans and the harlots go into the kingdom of God before you" (Matt. 21:31). When a woman caught in the very act of adultery was dragged before Him, He forgave her.

We speak of our receiving Christ, but we receive Him because He first received us. Careful scrutiny of Christ's genealogy in Matthew reveals a foreshadowing of His willingness to be linked with the socially inferior, the racial outsider, and sinners. He consented to be born into a line that specifically mentioned four women who in that culture were considered low on the social scale; two were Gentiles and the others guilty of adultery.

Because Christ came to save the lost, how fitting that He spent much time in the company of sinners. The occupation of tax-collector was held in deep disdain and linked with the lowest of the low. Hence the expression "publicans and sinners."

Yet our Lord called a publican to be one of His disciples and led him to author the first Gospel, Matthew. After his call to service, Matthew threw a big dinner to which he invited a large number of publicans and sinners—and Jesus, who accepted the invitation. As a result He was criticized because He ate and drank "with publicans and sinners" (Mark 2:16).

If an alcoholic persists in seeking help in the fellowship of some evangelical churches, he might find something less than a welcome. Before long he might find himself shoved off to the Salvation Army, the waterfront mission, or Alcoholics Anonymous. Yet Jesus so received sinners that He was called a man "gluttonous, and a winebibber," as well as "a friend of publicans and sinners" (Matt. 11:19). He did not participate in drunken revellings, which Scripture forbids to believers (1 Peter 4:3), but He did so associate with the intemperate that He was known as their Companion and Friend.

Does the average Christian today let himself get very close to or involved with unsavory characters, or does he rather pull his skirts of self-righteous separation about him and keep such sinful folks at proper distance? Much more Christlike was the gesture of then Deputy Inspector Conrad Jensen of the New York City police who one night was told by Jim Vaus, worker among East Harlem delinquents, that a gang leader by the name of Shane had accepted Christ that evening. Policeman Jensen, who knew Shane well, for he had often been in trouble with the law, put his arm around Shane and said, "That makes us brothers now."

Moody Monthly magazine carried the "Confession of a Pharisee" who along with two other church members lived in a lovely neighborhood where the only moral blot was Ada, a woman married to her second husband with whom she violently fought. The family brawls with their abusive language grew out of constant drinking. The three church members, all of whom lived across, next to, or around the corner from Ada and all of whom were Sunday School teachers or members of the Ladies Society, were ashamed to meet Ada on the street or in a store, for fear that, with reeking alcoholic breath or loud voice, she would introduce them as her friends. Not one of the women called on her. Then rumors began to circulate of Ada's serious illness. They planned to go over some time or ask her to lunch. They planned to tell her about Christ and invite her to church. But one day a hearse drew up to Ada's house. Ada had tried to quit liquor but couldn't. The confession ends, "The silent witness of that body on the stretcher will haunt us for a long time. Can one of us honestly say we cared for Ada's soul? That's why I say we three are Pharisees."

Since our Lord came to die for sinners, including thieves, how fitting He should die between thieves. Most people would not like their picture taken with a thief on either side. But people are proud to have their picture snapped with some celebrity. Yet every time the three crosses are depicted, Christ hangs between robbers.

James wrote about welcoming people into God's house. He wrote, in effect, "My brothers, don't hold the faith and be guilty of snobbery. If there come to the door of your church a man with a gold ring, well-dressed, and there also enters a poor man in patched clothing, and you shower attention on the well-dressed man and say, 'Here's a front seat for you,' but you shove the shabby fellow back in the corner, are you not then guilty of partiality?" (James 2:1-4). James knew full well that such discrimination was far removed from His Master's example.

Because the Lord Jesus Christ extended a loving welcome to outcasts, outsiders, and outlaws, every Christian is debtor to the lowest, the least, the last, and the lost.

6

"I'll Forgive, But I Won't Forget"

The murder of five young American missionaries by Auca Indians on a river bed deep in Ecuador's rain forest in 1956 startled the civilized world. Just as startling are some of the events since then. The widow of one of the missionaries and the sister of another moved into Auca territory to live unharmed among the very Indians who took the missionaries' lives. Among the first Auca men to believe the Gospel were the five killers, who since have all been baptized. During the two years these women lived there, it was not an uncommon sight to see the little blond daughter of one of the martyred missionaries being carried around in the arms of the man who murdered her father.

Nine years after the tragedy another widow of the martyred missionaries visited the beach where her husband had been speared. She was accompanied by her two sons, 16 and 14 years old, who were then baptized by the men who had killed their father in the very river by which their father had died.

Ten years after the tragedy, at the World Congress on Evangelism in Berlin, one of the murderers of the missionaries was a delegate and was introduced to the assembly by the sister of one of the martyrs. Perhaps people ask, "How could this sister and the widows treat so kindly these savages who were their loved ones' murderers?"

The answer is found in the teachings and example of the Lord Jesus Christ. Not only did He emphasize forgiveness, but He practiced it both during His ministry and through His redemptive work on the cross. Sacred writ exhorts the Christian to "meekness, long-suffering; forbearing one another, and forgiving one another, if any man have a quarrel against any" (Col. 3:12, 13). Then to buttress this virtue, the inspired record points to the example of the Master. "Even as Christ forgave you, so also do ye" (Col. 3:13). Christlikeness calls for a forgiving spirit.

CHRIST FORGAVE

The good news of the Gospel boils down to one word—forgiveness. Christ came to forgive. To the man sick with palsy He uttered these cheering words, "Thy sins be forgiven thee." He led the woman of Samaria who had had five husbands to joyful heart-cleansing. He absolved the woman taken in adultery, "Neither do I condemn thee; go, and sin no more" (John 8:11). He forgave Zaccheus his greed for gold and his fraudulent practices saying, "This day is salvation come to this house" (Luke 19:9).

CHRIST FORGAVE MUCH AND MANY

Not only did Christ forgive but He forgave repeatedly and magnanimously. He taught unlimited forgiveness. Peter once asked the Lord, "How oft shall my brother sin against me, and I forgive him?" Without waiting for an answer, Peter generously suggested "seven times," a number far in excess of the rabbinical teaching of three times. He scarcely could have anticipated the celestial arithmetic of forgiveness contained in Jesus' answer, "until seventy times seven."

We find it hard to forgive someone who hasn't listened to our instructions carefully the first time. When we scold, "Listen this time, for I won't repeat it," we virtually declare our unwillingness to forgive inattention more than once. Or we say, "I'll forgive you this once, but don't let it happen again!" But Jesus declared we should forgive 490 times, if necessary.

He once commanded the disciples to forgive the same person seven times in the same day, if requested. No wonder they responded, "Increase our faith" (Luke 17:4, 5)!

Toward His disciples who repeatedly argued as to who would be greatest in the kingdom, He exercised forgiving patience. Each time He tolerantly taught the same lesson of humility, finally demonstrating the lesson by washing their feet the night before He went to the cross.

When He mentioned at the Last Supper, "One of you shall betray Me," He spoke not only prophetically but also wooingly toward Judas, letting him know his dastardly deed was not concealed, yet magnificently keeping his identity secret.

About to be betrayed, denied, and forsaken, He prayed in the garden for those who would prove so unfaithful.

Even while Judas was in the very act of trickery, Jesus called the betrayer "friend" and let him smirch His holy cheek with a kiss. The divine arms were still open to bestow forgiveness should Judas have repented.

Would you feel kindly toward someone who fell asleep after you had specifically asked him to keep vigil with you during a critical situation? Would not your patience almost reach its limit if he dropped off to sleep a second time? In Gethsemane, Peter, James, and John fell asleep three times after Jesus had asked them to keep watch. Yet Jesus' remark, "Sleep on now, and take your rest" (Mark 14:41), if taken ironically is at most a mild rebuke, indicating forgiveness. If taken literally, an interval of time elapsed before the arrest, during which Jesus Himself watched over the drowsy disciples, who were too sleepy to watch over Him.

For the Pharisees, Sadducees, and Herodians who persistently opposed Him and plotted against His life, He reserved His invectives till the last week of His life. Always He answered their questions kindly. Even to the end He pled, taught, persuaded.

He held no malice against those arresting Him in the garden. Availability of full forgiveness for a whole gang was symbolized in His restoration of Malchus' ear, chopped off by impetuous Peter.

Against His rejectors He bore no grudge. Rejected but not resentful, He would gladly have received His detractors under His wings as a hen gathereth her chicks, had they been willing.

His first two words from the cross were cries of forgiveness. For those involved in His death He asked, "Father, forgive them, for they know not what they do." Above the babel of wicked voices came the sweet music of mercy. Hitherto quiet before His accusers, He now opens His mouth, not to curse, but to bless.

Not only did all participating in that wicked travesty receive temporary stay of execution from divine wrath, but thousands found forgiveness. The centurion a few hours later acknowledged Jesus as the Son of God. On the day of Pentecost, 3,000 believed, many of whom had joined in that chorus of mockery, "Crucify Him," 50 days before. Later a great company of priests also became obedient to the faith.

But first of all to be forgiven was the repentant thief. Sweeter words of remission never fell on erring heart, "Today shalt thou be with Me in paradise." The second utterance from the cross, like the first, was a word of forgiveness.

How often the Lord forgave Peter for his wavering ways! When the cock crowed twice after Peter's third denial, the Lord looked so pityingly at Peter that the denier's heart broke. In love the

Lord sought a private interview with Peter on the resurrection day. Later on the shore the Lord, in forgiving Peter for the three public denials, had him make three public affirmations of love.

At a camp meeting altar a Christian man threw his arms around a non-Christian who had just come forward and falling to his knees wept with the repentant man. What made the scene unusual was the fact that the Christian's wife had been taken from him by this non-Christian penitent. A far more normal response would have been for the offended man to punch the wife-stealer rather than embrace him. Yet for Christ's sake, because Christ had forgiven him much, he forgave much.

CHRIST TOOK THE INITIATIVE IN FORGIVENESS

Christ took the initiative in the matter of forgiveness. While enduring the cruelty of the crucifixion, Christ offered forgiveness, even in the absence of any specific request for pardon. Well before others sought remission He showed willingness to forgive.

He had taught that the injured party should take the first step toward reconciliation. "If thy brother shall trespass against thee, go and tell him his fault between thee and him alone; if he shall hear thee, thou hast gained thy brother" (Matt. 18: 15). If the injured party rebukes his trespasser seven times in one day, and the guilty culprit repents all seven times, the injured person must forgive him all seven times (Luke 17:3, 4).

One reason Christ showed by pattern and

precept that the offended party should take the initiative was to prevent resentment. Most persons if mistreated with a fraction of the indignity Christ suffered would rankle with bitterness toward their tormentors. Sometimes hurt feelings carry high price tags. They often backfire, causing indigestion, fatigue, insomnia, or carelessness, resulting in highway accidents or industrial mishaps. Someone has said, "What we eat may not harm us as much as what may be eating us."

So that grudges would not have time to be nursed into sulky self-pity or vengeful spite, Christ instructed His followers to air their grievances immediately. The sun should not go down upon our wrath. Christlikeness does not stand on its dignity, making the other fellow come around, but gets its complaint out of its system right away.

If an offending believer will not hear our rebuke, we are to approach him a second time with witnesses. If he remains adamant we are to tell it to the church, who will excommunicate him as a heathen (Matt. 18:15-17).

Naturally we cannot forgive if forgiveness is not sought. But we can be willing to forgive. Though the Lord pronounced judgment on the cities of Galilee which rejected His presence, He held out the offer of pardon. So willing was He to forgive Jerusalem that not only did He weep over it, but He delayed its destruction 40 years, giving its inhabitants a chance to repent.

A Christian woman told her doctor she was suffering from severe headaches. Noting her tenseness he asked a few routine questions. He discovered that her non-Christian husband made fun of her faith. He often brought trashy magazines into the living room to irritate her. Through wise counsel her Christian physician led her to see the harm of resentment. He pointed out the example of Christ who prayed for forgiveness for His tormentors. Pondering the pattern of Christ and permitting His indwelling presence to live out through her, she developed a forgiving spirit. Her headaches disappeared. Her husband mellowed toward the Gospel.

CHRIST PUT FORGIVENESS CENTRAL

Christ placed forgiveness central. The reason He came was not to condemn but to forgive. The elements of the Lord's Supper picture a body broken and blood shed for the forgiveness of sins. The Great Commission commands announcement of this good news of available forgiveness.

Christ delighted to forgive penitent publicans and sinners. The Pharisees who murmured at Jesus' welcome to outcasts missed the main purpose of His mission by failing to grasp the all-important attribute of pardoning love. Like the elder brother of the parable of the prodigal, self-righteous, cold and hard like steel, they were out of tune with fatherly forgiveness.

A person who refuses to forgive those who offend him reveals he has not experienced forgiveness. The only section of the Lord's prayer elaborated on was the clause on forgiveness. Immediately after the "amen," Jesus explained, "For if ye forgive men their trespasses, your heavenly Father will also forgive you. But if ye forgive not men their trespasses, neither will your Father forgive your trespasses" (Matt. 6:14, 15). This comment points out that a forgiving spirit is evidence of the Father's forgiveness. Failure to forgive indicates we have never received divine remission, else we would be merciful.

Three days before He died, in the shadow of the cross, Christ warned, "When ye stand praying, forgive, if ye have ought against any: that your Father also which is in heaven may forgive you your trespasses. But if ye do not forgive, neither will your Father which is in heaven forgive your trespasses" (Mark 11:25, 26).

In His parable of the merciless servant, the Lord used humorous exaggeration to drive home the indispensability of a forgiving spirit. A servant who owed his master a staggering debt, roughly equivalent to $10 million, about to be tossed into prison, begged for mercy and received it. But then the forgiven servant on his release refused a plea for mercy from a fellow servant who owed him the tiny debt of $10 and threw him into jail. On hearing the story the master who had at first remitted the $10 million debt reversed his initial cancellation of debt and threw the merciless servant into prison. Jesus ended the story, "So likewise shall My heavenly Father do also unto you, if ye from your hearts forgive not every one his brother their trespasses" (Matt. 18:35).

Refusal of the merciless servant to exercise mercy revealed his failure to realize the enormity of his debt and the vastness of the mercy extended him.

Our trespasses against Christ cannot be computed but stagger us with their magnitude. Our wrongs against Him are a million times greater than the wrong any human may do us. If we genuinely ask forgiveness of Christ for our million-size debt against Him, how can we refuse mercy to a fellow creature for his tiny-in-comparison harm against us? "Even as Christ forgave you, so also do ye." Refusal to forgive betrays a lack of comprehension of Christ's grace. An unforgiving spirit reveals an unforgiven spirit. But he who is forgiven much loveth much.

A man retorted, "I'll forgive him this time but never again!" What if Christ said the same to the forgiver, "I'll forgive you this time but never again"?

A woman said to her pastor, "I'll forgive Mrs. X, but I won't have anything to do with her. I don't want to see her again. I won't let her in my house!"

The pastor replied, "Suppose Christ treats you the same way, wants nothing to do with you, won't let you into His presence or heavenly home?"

How often people react, "I'll forgive, but I won't forget." Christ has both forgiven and remembered our sins no more. To remember a grievance betrays lack of full forgiveness. If we forgive, we must forget.

Sometimes tragedy makes people see the folly of holding resentment. During the San Francisco earthquake of 1906, a man running out on Market

Street where buildings reeled for 48 seconds met and shook hands with a man he had refused to speak to for 10 years.

Two missionaries, one German and one French, in an Asian country when World War 2 broke out between Germany and France, forgot their years of happy friendship. With dead prejudices revived, the two men became enemies, raising a wall of hostility. One afternoon they came to the mission chapel at the same moment to ring the bell for vespers. Reaching for the bell rope, their hands touched. Looking upward, they both gazed at the cross on top of the mission. Then they threw their arms around each other, asking forgiveness. The love of Christ symbolized by the cross had broken down the barriers.

An American airman was shot down by a Japanese pilot. Somehow the parents of the American youth discovered who the Japanese pilot was. They gave several thousand dollars to bring the Japanese youth to the U.S. and paid several thousands of dollars they had saved for their son's education to send this lad to a Pennsylvania university.

A shamefaced employee was summoned to the president's office. The least he expected was angry dismissal. At most he might have gotten years in prison for embezzling company funds. The old president asked, "Are you guilty?"

The clerk lowered his head, admitted his guilt, and added how sorry he was.

"I shall not press charges that might send you to prison. If I take you back, can I trust you?"

Surprised but melted, the clerk gave assurance of absolute honesty.

The president spoke slowly. "You're the second man who fell and was pardoned. I was the first. The mercy you just received I received. May God have mercy on us both."

Vengeance is the natural human attitude toward those who mistreat us. But Christ's example overturned such thinking. Contemplation of the cross where He forgave us so fully and freely should dislodge any grudges we have toward others. We can't receive His forgiveness and keep our feet on our brother's neck.

7

Humility of Heaven

World-famed evangelist Billy Graham donned a disguise and joined thousands of college students on the beach at Fort Lauderdale. Chatting with many of the young people, he moved in and out of the throngs who thought him just another collegian. None of the students recognized this internationally known celebrity, who humbly maintained his anonymity.

Infinitely greater condescension was displayed by the Celebrity of heaven in His coming to earth almost 2,000 years ago. The all-resplendent Christ surrendered His glory. He who was Deity became man. Master became servant. The Preeminent One of heaven became a nobody on earth. He who was Life suffered death. He who was spotlessly honorable suffered the shame of death on a Roman gibbet.

Humility is an elusive virtue. When we think we have it we've lost it! One religious order boasted, "Other groups may excel us in almsgiving, self-denial, or scholarship, but when it comes to humility, we're tops!"

Because self-assertive pride was the cause of disunity in the Philippian church, Paul urged them to do nothing through strife or vainglory. The cure for disharmony was humility. To vividly illustrate the lowliness of mind for which he was appealing, the apostle could point to no more majestic model than the Lord Jesus Christ, "who, being in the form of God, thought it not robbery to be equal with God; but made Himself of no reputation, . . . took upon Him the form of a servant, . . . was made in the likeness of men: . . . humbled Himself, and became obedient unto death, even the death of the cross" (Phil. 2:6-8).

Christ exhibited incomparable humility in His comedown from the highest to the lowest. From the throne of God He descended to the grave of man.

This series of classic clauses on the humiliation of Christ was not penned to prove subtle theological dogmas or teach minute mysteries, but to demonstrate a Christian duty. Contemplation of Christ's condescension should help us pour contempt on all our pride. A similar frame of mind in us would undercut dissension and create kind regard for others.

He Didn't Grasp After Glory

A wealthy woman generously offered to foot the bill for ice cream at a Sunday School picnic.

When little children's hands were eagerly reaching for the ice cream after supper, the woman became angry because no one announced that *she* was giving the money and petulantly refused to pay.

Instead of grabbing for vainglory this woman should have gazed on One who didn't grasp after true glory. Christ didn't esteem the honor of equality with God, which was rightfully His, a prize to be held at all cost.

Most men in high office like to be known as president of the company or chairman of the board. The flesh is easily irked when others fail to recognize our honorable position or when we aren't the center of attention. People enjoy posing for a picture with prominent persons and readily assert friendship with notable figures. But Christ didn't count the prestige of equality with God such a fascination that it had to be tenaciously retained and conspicuously spotlighted. He willingly gave it up to save us.

Though Christ laid aside the *expression* of His deity, He kept *possession* of it. He was always God, even when He didn't look like God to others. His glory was concealed, not lessened. Had He wished, He could have moved around Judea and Galilee with dazzling glory which would have felled people as it did the three disciples on the mount of transfiguration, the Apostle Paul on the Damascus road, and John on the Isle of Patmos.

But He chose to conceal His glory for 33 years. How quickly we should renounce vain show and conceited egotism, causes of so much dissension and meanness.

HE WHO WAS GOD BECAME MAN

He who was God became man. What happened that first Christmas was the reverse of what happened in the rise of many dictators and emperors. The Caesars ordered emperor-worship. Until World War 2 the Japanese emperor was revered as a man who became a god. Many dictators have mistaken themselves for a god, ranting and raving with supposed absolute power. In gross self-inflation these puny men proudly lifted themselves to what they were not, nor ever could be.

But in that Bethlehem cattle stall we have, not a man becoming God, but God in humility becoming man. Still retaining His deity the Lord Jesus Christ took on Him real human nature. He was born a baby. As a helpless infant He was carried by His parents in flight into Egypt.

His humility was reflected in His inglorious associations with outcasts, outsiders, and outlaws. He touched lepers, talked with demon-possessed, preached to the poor, ate with publicans and sinners, and died between thieves.

As a man He suffered the entire gamut of infirmities known to the race apart from sin. Though the Bread of Life, He knew what it was to be hungry. Though the Water of Life, He experienced thirst. He who invited the burdened to come to Him for rest became weary. He was lonely, despised, forsaken, mocked, lost a loved one in death, and passed through the valley of the shadow of death.

If the Creator of all left His exalted position to become a creature on earth, how quickly should we who are but creatures of dust come down off our haughty thrones.

HE WHO WAS MASTER BECAME SERVANT

A newly appointed board chairman of a large company visited a branch factory in a distant city. Applying incognito for a job, he donned working clothes and performed regular tasks along with the men in the factory. Though still top man in the corporation, he took orders as an employee among employees.

The Master of the universe, whose slightest bidding was immediately executed by myriads of angelic ministers, became a servant in His own creation. What a humiliating contrast for one accustomed to giving orders to take orders. It was as if the Queen of England should don overalls to sweep the street. Or a general stoop to K.P. duty. Or an admiral go below deck to stoke like a common seaman.

Members of the Indian Parliament once gave a tea party for their servants at a New Delhi hotel. Sitting with the Prime Minister were a sweeper, a butler, a gardener, and a watchman. Caste barriers were fractured as members of parliament served tea to the servants. Christ vividly illustrated His servanthood when He, the Lord of creation, removed His outer garments and stooped to wash His disciples' feet, a job usually performed by menial help.

HE WHO WAS LIFE DIED

Death is humiliating. Eyelids close. Ears no longer hear. The mouth no longer speaks, nor do hands work or feet walk. A corpse is an abject example of the utter weakness of human existence. How mortifying for the Lord of Life to die!

All things were made by Him, Giver and Sustainer of breath. As Resurrection and Life, He raised the dead on at least three occasions. Then He permitted Himself to die.

Pondering Christ's obedience to death should spur us to crucify our self life, especially pride. An important Christian leader dropped into a church service where an outstanding Bible teacher was preaching. The speaker spotted the church dignitary and meant to acknowledge his presence before the end of the meeting. But in the enthusiasm of preaching he forgot, so sent a telegram later to the leader, who wired back, "Dead. Didn't even notice it."

The late Gladys Aylward, known as the "Small Woman," said in an address to college students, "Are you thinking of going to the mission field for thrilling and romantic experiences? If so, don't come! They aren't there. It's following Jesus, step by step, from the graveyard of selfish ambitions into the life of God." The place to begin is at the cross where contemplation of His death leads to mortification of conceit.

In listing the downward steps of Christ's voluntary humiliation, Paul lingers on His death. How astonishing that God the Son should die! But all the more amazing that He should die the way He did! "Even the death of the *cross!*" Execution by crucifixion was reserved for the lowest of the low—slaves, criminals, outcasts—never for a Roman citizen. The Jews regarded it as an accursed death.

All the indignities heaped on Christ on His way to the cross compounded the ignominy. How abasing for the King of kings to be questioned by earthly governors as to His authority for His actions, to be made sport of, spit on, betrayed, stripped of His clothes three times, rejected while the people voted for the release of public enemy number one in preference to Himself, humiliated under the weight of the cross, crucified naked in public between criminals, wrapped in burial clothes, and laid in a sepulcher sealed by Roman authority.

He Who Was Somebody Became Nobody

His lowliness of mind is aptly summed up in this descriptive statement, "He made Himself of no reputation."

During graduation exercises at a well-known eastern university the large audience sat dutifully through the monotonous proceedings. Suddenly, the crowd jolted to attention, as if an electric shock had jarred everyone in the building. Walking down the aisle from a seat near the back, as his name was called, marched an erect five-star general of the army to receive an honorary degree. This top brass with all the dignity of his position commanded the rapt interest of all. But had he been dressed as a civilian and named without title, many would not have noticed.

Our Saviour, far above the five-star general-ship of heaven, came to earth without His insignia showing. Assuming the garb of humanity, He walked about on earth without people knowing who He was. Had you lived in Palestine you might have passed Him on a dusty road without the slightest inkling of His real person. A great artist paints a beautiful picture and is honored. Christ painted sunsets and scenes no human artist can begin to rival, yet as He walked around no one knew Him as the great Artist. A musician composes an oratorio and becomes famous; Christ made the music of the spheres and all music possible, yet as He moved from home to home, no one knew Him as the great Musician. Most school children know who discovered electricity; but He who made the suns was unsung. He knew all things, yet boasted no degrees after His name. He made Himself of no reputation.

When John Kennedy's son was born just before Kennedy's inauguration as president, com-munication systems around the world proclaimed the news to all. When the Christ-child was born midst the stable stench of an animal's feeding trough, no fireworks nor fanfare blared out His coming. An angelic message announced this stu-pendous news to a mere handful of humble herds-men. The circumstances of His birth doubtless made Him the butt of scandalous gossip.

His own brothers thought Him insane. His

opponents accused Him of possession by demons or partnership with the devil. He walked the paths of Israel unknown by people.

John D. Rockefeller, Jr., used to walk around Rockefeller Center when the tall building was in the process of construction. Farsighted, he could observe almost everything from the sidewalk. Once a watchman accosted him. "Move along, buddy," he growled. "You can't stand loafing here." Rockefeller quietly withdrew, unrecognized.

Jesus Christ, the great Somebody, made Himself a Nobody. It was said of Him, "There standeth One among you, whom ye know not." Even when those He healed wished to broadcast His exploits He ordered them to tell no one. Most people would have likely shifted their publicity machine into high gear.

He came to His own but His own received Him not. Shoved like a chess piece back and forth across a board, He became a pawn between governors Pilate and Herod. His final rejection, climaxed by His degrading death, He termed as being "set at nought" (Mark 9:12). He became a nothing. Feature the Infinite lowered to a zero. No wonder Andrew Murray once termed humility the secret of redemption.

The depth of Christ's descent contrasted violently with the vainglorious Pharisees who, to show off before men, prayed on street corners, trumpeted before giving, and disfigured their faces when fasting. Humility, not hypocrisy, should characterize our lives.

A rider on horseback during the Revolutionary

War came across a squad of soldiers trying to move a heavy piece of timber. A corporal stood by with a self-important air, giving lordly orders to "heave." But the piece of timber was a trifle too heavy for the squad.

"Why don't you help them?" asked the quiet man on the horse, addressing the corporal.

"Me? Why, I'm a corporal, sir!"

Dismounting, the stranger carefully took his place with the soldiers. "Now, all together, boys, heave!" he exclaimed. And the big piece of timber slid into place.

The stranger mounted his horse. Then turning to the corporal, he said, "Next time you have a piece of timber for your men to handle, Corporal, send for the commander-in-chief." The horseman was George Washington!

Love of applause, vain show, and the pride of life rear their haughty heads in modern life. Church members sometimes take offense when their deeds fail to receive public acknowledgment, or when their names aren't printed in the church annual for some special service. A worshiper readied a dollar bill in his hand at offering time in a fashionable church. When he noted that the usher coming down the aisle was an important business acquaintance, he replaced the dollar in his pocket and removed a $20 bill, waving it as he dropped it on the plate.

Usually far more money is promised during network telethons for charitable causes than ever is finally contributed. People like to hear their names mentioned over TV. Some employees have pretended patriotism by purchasing war bonds at work, then almost immediately quietly sold them. Some people always want to be running the show, or sitting at the head table.

Humility was never an admired virtue in the ancient world. In a day that stressed self-assertiveness, humility was usually regarded as the despised opposite of courage. For a person to fail to stand up for his rights betrayed weakness to the secular mind. But Christ by His supreme example of self-abasement reversed this mood. He established humility as a lofty virtue, and He condemned pride along with murder and adultery.

If we would have the mind of Christ we must ponder often His example of self-effacement which made Him leave the ivory palaces to sink to this world of woe. Possession of this mental disposition led one church member to give to a new church edifice with this instruction, "Use this gift in unseen parts of the building. You can find enough people who want to give their money for parts that can be seen."

8

Jesus, the Gentleman

A woman who was expecting a baby any day moved to a new area where her husband worked nights. Her only neighbor assured her, "My husband will drive you to the hospital should you have to go in the middle of the night."

After midnight on a windy night the expectant mother rang her neighbor's bell to arouse them. The wife opened the door. "Oh, I'm sorry but my husband can't take you to the hospital. But come in while I call a cab!"

Not till after the safe arrival of the baby did the new mother learn what had happened. Her husband brought her a note he had found at his front door on returning from work at dawn. It read, "I'm sorry my husband was not here to drive your wife to the hospital. He passed away of a heart attack yesterday. I did not want to tell your wife, for I was afraid it would upset her."

Despite the grief tearing at her heart, the

bereft wife displayed kind consideration. The prominent trait in Christ's personality was His gentleness. He was called the *Lamb* of God. Not only was He King of kings and Lord of lords, but Gentleman of gentlemen.

Because the Apostle Paul did not bully nor browbeat but conducted himself meekly and considerately, his enemies accused him of weakness and contemptible speech. In defense of his mild manners Paul pointed to the example of Jesus, "Now I Paul myself beseech you by the meekness and gentleness of Christ . . ." (2 Cor. 10:1). His appeal to this quality not only explained his seeming timorous behavior but indirectly urges Christians today to meek and gentle conduct.

Meekness is not weakness, nor is it Milquetoast timidity. Rather it is strength grown gentle. The stevedore who, after tossing huge crates around the wharf, goes home to handle his five-month-old baby tenderly has not become weak. He has toned down his strength to gentleness.

The gentleness of Jesus was all the more remarkable when etched against His strength. Despite the impression of paintings which make Him effeminate, insipid, sentimental, and on the verge of tears, He was vigorous and strong. His manliness attracted robust and rough Galilean sailors. His courageous scorn made Him dangerous enough to be crucified.

Because His righteous anger flashed out against Pharisaical injustice, His gentleness was never soft nor flabby but lined with steel. Against the background of His scathing indignation at the

Pharisees who in hardness of heart did not want to see a man healed on the Sabbath, stood out His tenderness to the unfortunate fellow with the withered hand. Someone has said, "He was gentle as only the fiercest can be gentle." The essence of gentleness lies in the curbing of strength to avoid injury to the weak. Our Lord did this with a tenderness that was never weak and with courage never brutal.

Many people picture a gentleman as an aristocrat with a monocle, stovepipe hat, striped trousers, cane, and Victorian manners. But the New Testament word for *gentleness* can be rendered *forbearance, consideration, sweet reasonableness,* or *mildness.* Two drivers, a man and a woman, tried to be first away on a green light. The man was heading straight, while the woman wanted to make a left turn across his lane. It was a tie with bumpers barely touching. But neither would back up, both insistent on right of way. Cars jammed up for five blocks in four directions from the intersection. When police arrived, both drivers were sitting silently but stubbornly behind their respective wheels. Had gentleness prevailed, each driver would have sweetly, mildly, and reasonably yielded right of way to the other.

So gentle was the Lord that it was declared, "A bruised reed shall He not break, and smoking flax shall He not quench, till He send forth judgment unto victory" (Matt. 12:20).

A reed, a frail plant so unlike the firm oak, though already bruised and with vitality sapped, He would not finish breaking. Those bowed down with penitent unworthiness and bruised feeble by the blows of life, the tender Christ would not injure more nor destroy, but would rather strengthen their delicate life.

When a lamp wick began to burn dimly and smoke thickly, the tendency was to quickly extinguish it. But when the flame flickered in the hearts of those on the verge of spiritual extinction, the mild Christ would not blow even softly lest He snuff out the dying flame. He never broke anyone's spirit.

TENDER IN DEED

A woman with a city-wide reputation as a sinner came unbidden into Simon the Pharisee's house where Jesus was a dinner guest and began to wash His feet with her tears and wipe them with her hair. The emotional warmth must have been embarrassing. But not only did He treat her kindly, but also defended her against Simon's cynicism (Luke 7:37-40).

The woman who was dragged to the feet of Jesus by the Pharisees who seized her in the very act of adultery must have stung under their accusations. How gently Jesus relieved her shame. After challenging those without sin to cast the first stone, He stooped to write something in the sand. His action turned attention away from the humiliated woman and permitted the convicted Pharisees to slip away one by one (John 8:6).

Many were the occasions when He set Himself between public sinners and the accusing finger of society, or came to the defense of the vulnerable.

How courteous He was to Judas, hiding his identity as traitor almost to the end. Most of us would have frankly named him but Jesus spared his feelings. At the arrest Jesus even called him "Comrade" and permitted the betrayer to kiss Him.

When helpless mothers with infants in arms were turned away from Jesus by gruff disciples, He rebuked the disciples and took the babies in His arms. Ruskin once observed that there were no children in Greek art, but that Christian art abounds with children. The prophet had declared that He would "gather lambs with His arm and carry them in His bosom and shall gently lead those that are with young" (Isa. 40:11).

His first miracle relieved the predicament of a young couple whose wedding refreshments ran short. How embarrassing if word got round, "Not enough drink for the wedding. Why, they couldn't really afford to get married!" Perhaps extra guests had come in from the country. The Lord graciously performed the miracle secretly so that even the host was surprised. The only people who knew about the miracle were the servants who also knew about the problem.

Mary was accused of waste by the disciples for anointing Jesus with a considerable quantity of expensive ointment. Knowing she had done this with keen insight as advance burial ministration, the Lord defended her action. Some clergymen might have given a sermon against the misuse of money, a far cry from Jesus' gentle approval.

A major temptation of the strong is impatience

with the weak and righteous contempt of the erring. But the strong Son of God extended His most gracious love to the frailest sinners who turned in His direction.

Accommodating consideration was shown the timid Nicodemus who came by night for an interview.

How gentle the Lord was in pointing out to the Samaritan woman that she had had five husbands. Some personal workers would have immediately begun the conversation with "You're a wicked woman!" But the Lord started with the request for a drink of water, then gently swung into her past. So kind was His approach she didn't mind that He told her all things ever she did (John 4:29).

As Jesus walked with Zacchaeus toward his home after inviting Himself for dinner, the stunned crowd murmured that He was gone to be guest with a notorious sinner. As the murmuring buzzed more loudly it became embarrassing not only to the crooked tax-collector but to Jesus, whose reputation was in danger of being soiled by association with a seemingly unrepentant publican. Some of us would have been tempted to lecture Zacchaeus on his need for restitution and charity, but Jesus patiently gave him a chance to express himself. His moderate treatment paid off as Zacchaeus announced his intent to make amends.

Frankness can be unnecessarily and brutally blunt at times. But the Lord combined mildness with His firmness.

Too often we react with fire against the slow-thinking and skeptical. But to weeping Mary in the garden He feelingly spoke her name. He sparred in genial conversation with the discouraged Emmaus disciples, patiently leading them to renewed faith in Himself. To doubting Thomas, He extended an invitation to put his finger in the nailprints, willing to submit to Thomas' prestated test.

Many of His physical gestures revealed gentleness. How often He tenderly touched the sick as He healed.

In cleansing the Temple He whipped out the money changers, sheep, oxen, dumped out the changers' money, and overturned the tables. But He didn't drive out the doves. Rather He said to those selling doves, "Take these things hence" (John 2:16), rather than harass those sensitive birds.

When He healed a man with a speech impediment, He took the victim aside from the crowd, perhaps to spare his feelings by providing privacy for his first attempts to speak plainly (Mark 7:32, 33).

MILD IN SPEECH

Gentleness controlled Christ's speech. Do you ever yell at your children or others? Do you ever shout at clerks or the driver who cuts you off? Ever raise your voice at your husband or your employees? Ever hear people loud in conversation?

Though on rare occasions the Lord did shout some important truth (John 12:44), His voice was usually conversational. Isaiah had predicted His soft-spokenness: "He shall not strive, nor cry; neither shall any man hear His voice in the streets" (Matt. 12:19). He was patient with His disciples, permissive with those undecided, and polite to His enemies.

His forbearance must often have been tested by the slowness of His disciples to learn. Yet He didn't fume at them, but kindly asked, "Do ye not yet understand?" Then He would meekly repeat His instruction.

How easy in trying to persuade others to our way of thinking to become argumentative, harsh, and authoritarian. But the Lord never strove but was gentle unto all men, meekly and patiently instructing those that opposed the truth. His invitations to conversion and consecration were always permissive. Though grieved when the rich young ruler turned away, He didn't pressure him into remaining.

Christlikeness in speech demands courtesy and kindness. This is why Paul referred the proudly assertive false teachers at Corinth to the meekness and gentleness of Christ.

COMPASSIONATE IN HEART

Christ's gentleness in deeds and words stemmed from His tenderness of heart. Able to share another's brokenness, the compassion of Christ radiated in every direction, toward those in pain, the poor, the plaintive, and the potentially penitent.

Our emotions are often jaded. A fictitious

couple about to be married in a soap opera received loads of presents delivered by truck after truck to station headquarters in New York. Yet some couples about to be married in real life, living around the corner from some sentimentalists, receive nothing. We weep over imaginary characters and their plight in fiction plots but steel our cold and calloused hearts against people in real-life distress who live in our neighborhoods. Christlikeness produces concern over lost souls.

A preacher was visiting in another church. A man remarked, "Our people are a most united church." When the preacher commended the church, the man warned, "Just a minute; don't praise us anymore till you hear the kind of unity we have. Our members are frozen together!"

Some people of Jesus' day thought He was Jeremiah, the weeping prophet. If others are to see Jesus in us, our attitude will have to be possessed by His compassionate gentleness.

Several times the Gospel writers specifically mention Christ's compassion for the ill. He was intensely moved by the sufferings of invalids, the palsied, the lame, the leprous, the maimed, the deaf, the dumb, the blind.

Though He had great power at His disposal, He never used it for His own safety or comfort. More than two-thirds of His miracles were performed for the relief of those sick in body or mind.

He was keenly sensitive to the plight of widows, the poor, and the needy. Because He had compassion on the hungry, He fed the multitude. He didn't scold the crowd about their lack of

foresight in following Him around without sufficient provisions, nor did He accept the disciples'
suggestion to send them away. Rather, He fed
them.

The sorrows of others always touched the
Saviour's heart. When the Lord raised the dead it
wasn't for the sake of the deceased, for they were
far better off in heaven than back on earth. His
sovereign purposes, along with compassion for the
bereaved, led Him to restore life. When He raised
Jairus' daughter and the widow of Nain's son, His
pity was doubtless intensified in each case by the
child's status as an only daughter and an only son.
How often He was moved by the implorings of a
parent for a child, sometimes an only child (Luke
9:38).

Loss over the death of Lazarus plus sympathy
for Mary and Martha caused Him to weep at the
grave (John 11:35). Even though He knew He
was about to exercise the power of His deity by
calling Lazarus forth from the tomb, the tears of
gentle humanity trickled down His holy cheeks.

When we see vast crowds of people hurrying
by some busy intersection, how do we react? Our
Lord saw the multitudes as scattered sheep without
a shepherd, lost, astray. He was moved with compassion over them (Matt. 9:36).

During His ministry He lamented over
Jerusalem. "How often would I have gathered thy
children together, as a hen doth gather her brood
under her wings, and ye would not!" (Luke 13:34)

Less than a week before He died, on His so-
called triumphal entry into Jerusalem, He shed

profuse tears over the city's fate (Luke 19:41).

A man who fractured a bone in his foot found it necessary to hobble around with a cane for several days. People helped him into buses, opened doors for him, and made room for him in elevators. But when he recovered sufficiently to leave the cane at home, people returned to their old jostling selves. Who knows how many folks are walking the streets every day who have frail emotional bones that have been broken and who need gentle treatment from others?

The healthy should picture what life is like looking out from the walls of a sickroom. The successful should ask how it feels to be under-privileged and underfed. The mature should remember that once they were young and filled with misgivings. Youth should put themselves in the place of the aged shut-in and disillusioned. Those blessed with brains should imagine what it would be like going through life with dull thinking. The moral should visualize life as an outcast.

Recently a Christian young man went to col-lect the rent from a couple who lived in a house he owned. He found the husband dying of an in-curable disease. He was in such bad shape that the young man would not take the rent money. Rather, he went home and wept because of the man's desperate condition. Then he notified the church where the man was a member so members could help him.

Are you brusque in your dealings with people? Do you run roughshod over their feelings?

Christlikeness should make us gentle as doves.

9

In the Hour of Trial

Jesus promised persecution to His followers. He warned that they would be betrayed by relatives, hated of all men, delivered to councils, scourged in public, tried before governors and kings, and even put to death (John 16:1-4; Matt. 10:17 ff). In fact, those who hounded His followers would think they were doing God a favor. No wonder Jesus foretold, "In the world ye shall have tribulation" (John 16:33).

Most of the apostles died violently as martyrs. Paul's sufferings in behalf of Christ are cataloged in detail (2 Cor. 11:20-29). In the extracanonical letter of the Smyrneans, a church for whom severe affliction had been predicted (Rev. 2:10), a tribute is paid to the noble and patient loyalty of their martyrs. Then a brief description follows, "seeing that when they were so torn by lashes that the mechanism of their flesh was visible even as far as the inward veins and arteries, they endured patiently, so that the very bystanders had pity and wept." Then follows a detailed account of the death of the aged Polycarp, Bishop of Smyrna, who, burning at the stake, praised Christ midst the flames.

Well known are the afflictions of the saints at Rome who were beheaded, fed to beasts in the arena, or used as human torches to light the way for the infamous Nero to ride to the coliseum.

Through the centuries Christians have met cruel treatment. *Fox's Book of Martyrs* contains voluminous records of the final agonies of harassed saints under brutal and inhuman torture.

Modern times have witnessed widespread martyrdom. One religious publication stated that there were more martyrs in the 19th century than in all previous centuries put together. No one knows the complete toll in Russia, Korea, China, and Colombia.

Christianity Today, commenting that one of the most tragic but least known aspects of the war in Vietnam has been the suffering inflicted upon Christian workers there, reported the murder of one of the country's leading Protestant pastors. After preaching in his own church in the Central Highlands one March Sunday morning, he was on his way to another service when he was overtaken by five armed men clad in black Viet Cong garb. He was killed on the spot, leaving his pregnant wife and eight children.

Three weeks later when a military school at Dalat was attacked, 17 chaplains were killed, many of them leaving wives and children.

Most Christians in the English-speaking world

know little or nothing of persecution. Perhaps ridicule, mockery, charges of obscurantism or puritanism have been leveled at us, but not bodily harm. Perhaps the day will come when Christians, even in America, will have to stand up firmly and be counted in the face of persecution.

If persecution comes, we have a supreme example of how to bear it. Martyrs of all ages have been strengthened by the perfect pattern of faith in the hour of trial, the Lord Jesus Christ. We are told to look to Him who for the joy set before Him endured the cross and despised the shame (Heb. 12:1-3).

We should make sure, however, that opposition from others is not our fault. We should neither court opposition nor develop persecution complexes. Some people excuse their poorly attended church services on the ground that their church preaches the Gospel. Some claim they can't get news releases into the papers about their Sunday Schools because they preach the Bible, and papers don't like the Bible. Maybe—there is an offense of the Gospel, but there is no need to be offensive in its presentation. Though some will be repulsed by the Gospel, we need not be repulsive in our manners. We are to be as winsome as possible, not carrying a chip on our shoulders.

A young person who carries a Bible to school, but who cheats on tests, fools his teachers and laughs with others at his cleverness, or skips classes and signs his parent's name on a note of excuse, will cause others to ridicule him. Their mockery is not at the Gospel but at the young Christian's inconsistency. We are to be wise as serpents and harmless as doves. We are to make sure that persecution that comes our way is for the Gospel's sake, not for our lack of tact, poor manners, or idiosyncrasies.

THE LORD JESUS SUFFERED

The Epistle to the Hebrews was written to Jews who had made a profession of Christ but who were in danger of turning back to Judaism. What was slowing them down was affliction, reproach, the spoiling of their property (Heb. 10:32-34). To encourage them the writer points to characters who through faith weathered obstacles to win major victories. These historical personages are catalogued in the famous gallery of heroes in Hebrews 11. But the supreme example of faith in the face of opposition is Jesus Christ with whom the writer begins the 12th chapter of Hebrews. The Lord Jesus Christ is the leader of faith over all other examples of faith. We are to consider Him, who endured the cross, despised the shame, keeping in view the heavenly reward which He now permanently enjoys (Heb. 12:1-3).

The Lord Jesus Christ suffered the contradiction of sinners, the cross, and contempt.

Contradiction of Sinners

A university president, whose job demanded the procurement of large gifts for the school, radiated charm and affability. Because a new young professor often blurted out the truth rather bluntly, the president diplomatically invited the young professor to a chapel service. The president spoke on the theme of how Jesus found common ground with His hearers to win them to His way. After the service the young professor thanked the president. "I shall try to profit by your address. But one thing bothers me. If Jesus was so beautifully tactful and diplomatic, how did He manage to get Himself crucified?"

Christ's claims were defiantly rejected from the beginning. His hometown people tried to push Him over a cliff (Luke 4:27-30). He was accused of blasphemy because He made Himself equal with God (John 10:33). He was accused of insanity (Mark 3:21) and of partnership with Beelzebub. His brothers disbelieved Him (John 7:3-5).

He was criticized because His disciples plucked corn (Matt. 12:1-9) and because He healed on the Sabbath (Luke 13:14). He was derided by covetous Pharisees (Luke 16:14). Continually the Pharisees tried to entangle Him in His talk. The Sadducees asked Him one of their trick questions. A lawyer tested Him with a question. The Herodians tried to trap Him. He was charged with letting the disciples transgress the tradition of the elders. His authority was questioned. He was murmured at because of His association with publicans and sinners (Luke 15:1).

The opposition became vehement (Luke 23:10). It culminated in His arrest and trial, where He was mocked as a make-believe king with crown of thorns, reed, and gorgeous robe. In loud chorus the chief priests and scribes cried out, "Away with this man. Crucify Him!" A hail of mockery was hurled at Him in His final agonies. He was betrayed by one of the Twelve, denied by another, and forsaken by all.

Cross

Painful indeed were the sufferings of crucifixion. These were preceded by the cruel scourge, a whip with leather pieces or bits of metal which would bite deeply into the flesh. Brought down brutally on the bare back, this whip would often lash around to dig into the face.

Physical taunts added to the pain, as soldiers smote Him, asking Him to prophesy who it was that did the striking. They also spat on Him.

The victim was often nailed to the cross flat against the ground. Soldiers would hold one hand, then the other, while a spike was driven through the palm, spurting blood. Lifted up into a hole in the ground, the victim would be jarred and jolted in every bone in his body. Then would follow hours of the excruciating tortures of crucifixion.

Because He was omniscient, the Lord suffered from the anticipation of this ordeal all during His ministry. He repeatedly foretold His sufferings. How greatly would our anticipatory knowledge torment us if we knew that in six months we would be nailed to a tree!

Shame

Added to the cruelty was shame. His kind of death was reserved for criminals and slaves — the death of the cross. His sufferings were compounded by disgrace.

Today we honor the emblem of the cross. But in His day wearing a cross would have been the equivalent of wearing a gallows, electric chair, or a gas chamber in our day. The Romans would have laughed had someone said that the cross would be an ornament someday. Christ's glorious sufferings have transformed the shame into glory.

The Lord Jesus Endured His Sufferings

The Lord's sufferings did not cause Him to falter or turn back. Rather He endured them. In this He is an example to us. If He bore such great opposition, pain, and shame, we should follow suit, especially since our sufferings have never been so intense. We have not resisted to the point of giving our life's blood. In the face of Calvary our tribulations should appear light. He is the supreme Exemplar of affliction-enduring faith. The Captain of our salvation never wavered.

He Endured the Contradiction

In the face of unwarranted hostility He sometimes was silent; often He gave a defense of His position. On the cross when urged to save Himself, He was quiet. Yet He spake so boldly to the high priest at His trial, that He was struck by an officer. But Jesus never apologized. Paul urges Timothy to fight the good fight of faith in view of the good confession which Christ witnessed before Pilate (1 Tim. 6:13). How often He defended Himself before the verbal onslaughts of His enemies, routing them completely.

He Endured the Cross

The cross meant physical and spiritual pain to Christ. Yet He patiently underwent it. His example should animate us. "For it is better, if the will of God be so, that ye suffer for well doing, than for evil doing. For Christ also hath once suffered for sins, the just for the unjust, that He might bring us to God" (1 Peter 3:17, 18).

> Lord, should my path through
>   suffering lie,
> Forbid it I should e'er repine,
> Still let me turn to Calvary,
> Remembering Thine.

He Esteemed the Shame As Nothing

He despised the shame. He regarded the ridicule as nothing in view of the glorious outcome.

Harassed believers are urged to look unto Jesus, turning away from all other things to make Christ the object of reflection (Heb. 12:2). The next verse again tells believers to consider Christ (v. 3). Analyze Him. Enter into His spirit. As He acted, we are to act. Contemplation of Him should dispel a fainting spirit.

We are to look unto Him not only as the perfecter of our faith but as the captain of our faith, leading us to imitate Him in this contest. We are to follow the leader. He didn't quit the race but stayed through every obstacle. If we are discouraged, a reminder of Him, the grandest portrait in the gallery of faith's heroes, should help us persist through bitter anguish to win the prize.

News out of China tells how in one area where

Christian leaders were suspected of loyalty to the Gospel, 30 pastors were called together. All who promised never to preach the Gospel again were asked to stand to one side. Two forsook the faith, but the other 28 stood firm. Then these 28 were taken out and shot.

A letter to someone in Hong Kong came out of Red China from a Christian. On one side of the envelope was the address, but on the other side was John 3:16 written out in Chinese. Two stamps were affixed, one on each side, so that those who had to check the stamps could not escape seeing John 3:16. The Christian inside Red China was giving a testimony to his faith in a way which risked his life. He was enduring.

A news report captioned, "It's not easy to be a Christian in East Berlin," related how in East Germany the government brought pressure on Christian families to send their children to Communist youth dedication ceremonies instead of having them confirmed in the church. If the child went to confirmation, he was barred from further education in the state-controlled schools. Sometimes the father was fired from his job on some flimsy pretext. Many gave in to such pressure, but those who remained true did not sneak into services, but walked proudly down the main street Sunday mornings, carrying Bible and hymnbook conspicuously.

A new schoolteacher in a suburban New York school testified that three years ago he was a non-Christian living in Colombia. His conversion stemmed from seeing the steadfastness of an evangelical pastor who had been beaten for preaching the Gospel in a remote area. The pastor's face was beaten black on one side, yet he rejoiced that he could suffer for Christ. He never registered a complaint. That started the young teacher thinking. Later he became a Christian. His family turned against him. To leave Colombia for America he had to sell his books.

Not only should the Christian in persecution not retaliate, but he should joyfully and patiently endure. A commander in the U.S. Navy stood on the outskirts of a crowd when General Eisenhower visited Paris some years ago. A mob of Communists was demonstrating against the coming of the American president as well as against NATO. Police arrested a large group of people, including the commander. He spent three hours in jail before he could explain he was an American curiously looking on, and not a Communist. While he was in jail a significant thing happened. He said these Communists began to sing and shout and were absolutely thrilled that they had the privilege of suffering for Communism. We need the same devotion to Christ, like Paul and Silas who sang praises at midnight.

THE LORD JESUS WAS REWARDED

Jesus found incentive to endure criticism, the cross, and the shame because of the anticipated reward. He "for the joy that was set before Him endured the cross" (Heb. 12:2).

He knew He would be raised from the dead,

exalted to the Father's right hand (v. 3), dispense salvation to those who would believe on Him, ultimately ruling and reigning, defeating Satan. The joy of anticipating a triumphant outcome gave Him courage.

The joy of future reward, if an incentive to Christ, is certainly a legitimate, though not the chief, motive for us to endure tribulations. The eternal glory makes the present trial seem but for a moment.

Paul knew that 'if deliverance did not come sometime from beating or imprisonment that there would be an ultimate, final deliverance through resurrection. He knew that when the executioner's sword fell, there would be yet another chapter. He would be raised someday. So knew all the apostles. This is why Peter could sleep the night before his scheduled execution. Jesus promised great reward to those who suffered for righteousness' sake (Matt. 5:11, 12).

An adventure story involves complication, then climax. Obstacles appear which are overcome in a grand and glorious solution. A little girl used to ask her daddy to tell a story, "What's got trouble in it but the trouble comes out all right." For the Christian there may be trouble, but someday it will be overcome.

> It will be worth it all when we see Jesus;
> Life's trials will seem so small when
> we see Christ;
> One glimpse of His dear face,
> all sorrow will erase;
> So bravely run the race, till we see Christ.

A famous preacher used to tell the story of two boys. One, known to be very bad, used to throw mud at the moon. The other, a very good boy, took a basin of water and tried to wash it off. What was the moon doing all the while? It just kept shining! When troubles come our way, whether or not anyone comes to our defense, let's just keep enduring and shining.

10

Joyful Jesus

Suppose Jesus were to enter a room and find a group of people laughing—what would happen? Many would answer, "Either the people would stop laughing or Jesus would give them a lecture against levity."

Sometimes a solemn person in a home where youthful members begin to indulge in merriment will retreat to a gloomy corner. The peals of laughter that ring out from happy youth will be punctuated by melancholy sighs from that dark corner.

Severe persons point out that Jesus never laughed. At least no such record exists. But He did weep on at least three occasions. He was a man of sorrows and acquainted with grief. Thus, mirth must be avoided in our lives, so they conclude.

But they fail to recognize that a large proportion of the four Gospels is devoted to the last week of Jesus' life. Almost one-third of the 89 chapters in Matthew, Mark, Luke and John deal with the tragic events of those final days. Increasing animosity, betrayal, arrest, trial, scourging, crucifixion, and burial create a solemnity of spirit for a large segment of the Gospel record. They also forget that the Lord lived 33 years before that climactic week, three years of which are covered by the four writers. In contrast to the serious atmosphere of the passion week stands out the lighthearted gladness so evident in His public ministry. Before the sad days were sunny years.

The Gospel record begins with joy: announcement of the gladness to Zacharias, songs of Elizabeth and Mary, messages of angels, happy shepherds, praise by Simeon and Anna, and the delight of the wise men at the reappearance of the star. The Gospel story ends with the disciples returning to Jerusalem with great joy after the ascension, where they continually blessed God in the temple. In between we have the delineation of One who was sociable, friendly, sunny, optimistic, cheerful, serene, self-possessed, peaceful, poised, calm, content, thankful, praiseful, who for the joy that was set before Him endured the cross. The Lord Jesus Christ was as much a man of joy as a man of sorrows.

This joy He wanted His followers to have. On the way to Gethsemane He said to His disciples, "These things have I spoken unto you, that My joy might remain in you, and that your joy might be full" (John 15:11). In the garden He prayed, "And now come I to thee; and these things I speak in the world, that they might have My joy fulfilled in themselves" (John 17:13). He referred to Himself as a model of joy. He wanted His followers to experience this same joy to the full. Since joy is listed second in the catalog of the fruit of the Spirit, right after love, and since Christ had the Spirit without measure, He must have been a joyful man. One commentator referring to these verses said, "Joy is attainable by careful imitation of His example. He revealed to His disciples by precept and example that the path of duty is the only path of joy. After obedience comes joy." The person who obeys the voice of Christ will radiate His joy.

He Was Sociable With Everyone

Jesus has been described as the most popular dinner guest in Jerusalem and Galilee. The newly converted Matthew threw a feast for publicans and sinners to which he invited Jesus. When Pharisees invited Jesus for dinner, He accepted their hospitality (Luke 7:36 and 11:37). Some of His instruction was given when a guest at dinners (Luke 14:1-24). He readily entered into the common joys of dining with people and the enjoyable relaxation such fellowship provides. In fact, His happy nature, wholesome enjoyment, and exuberant participation gave Him the reputation among His enemies of "a man gluttonous, and a winebibber" (Matt. 11:19). Though not intemperate He was a delight to have around. He was sociable, not ascetic. His initial miracle was performed at a wedding in Cana. Had He been as solemn as some people make Him out to be, on hearing of the shortage of refreshments, He might have austerely replied, "We've had enough merriment for one day. A few months ago I was hungry in the wilderness for 40 days. It would be better if we all practiced self-discipline. We wish the couple a prosperous life. Now let us all go home!" But He performed a miracle and kept the party going.

Jesus was criticized by the Pharisees because He and His disciples didn't look gloomy enough, especially when John the Baptist and his followers had been so solemn (Luke 5:33). His reply was that His presence required joy just as when a bridegroom joins a wedding party (Luke 5:34). The Lord forbade pretentious solemnity (Matt. 6:16). What a contrast must have been evident between the long faces of the legalistic Pharisees and the cheerful countenance of the relaxed Christ.

So often in teaching, the Lord represented Gospel blessings under the figure of a dinner. In the parable of the wise and foolish virgins the kingdom of heaven was likened to a marriage feast (Matt. 25:1-13). A famous painting portraying our Lord with the Twelve is called "The Last Supper." Jesus' final invitation in the four Gospels is "Come and dine" (John 21:12). One of the two church ordinances is known as "The Lord's Supper." The delights of saints united with Christ in heaven is termed "the marriage of the Lamb" (Rev. 19:7), and fulfills Christ's promise to His disciples to eat and drink at His table in His kingdom (Luke 22:30). Likeness of the Gospel to a supper conveys the idea of joyful fellowship, not melancholy. It was the elder brother who remained outside the merriment of the feast given in ecstasy over the return of the prodigal, which showed that the elder brother was out of tune with his father's joy and was the real problem.

Far from shunning the society of men or condemning the common joys, the Lord had a zest for life which made Him take note of the beauty of landscapes, flowers, storms, birds, lakes, mountains, sunrise, the play of children, the beauty of the temple, the work of farmers, fishermen, vinedressers, judges, and servants.

It's not unlikely that His lighthearted friendliness helped attract people from all ranks of life, from the top of the social ladder to the bottom. From the upper levels there were Nicodemus, the wife of Herod's treasurer, and later Joseph of Arimathea; from the middle class, fishermen, soldiers, lawyers; from the lower rungs, lepers, publicans, sinners, and the Samaritans who strongly desired Him to stay in their area (John 4:40). What a spectacle to see this motley group trailing Jesus through the streets and countryside! A certain radiant, magnetic buoyancy must have emanated from His person to draw disciples so readily. Children ran to Him. Lower classes did not feel uneasy in His presence. Those who squirmed were hypocritical leaders with entrenched privilege. Crowds received Him gladly. His friends enjoyed every minute of His stay in their homes. He must have often been a guest in the home of Mary, Martha, and Lazarus. Most evenings during His final week He retired to their Bethany home to fortify Himself for the stresses of the next day.

A religious leader decided not to ask the blessing at dinner because just before and after grace his
family would be laughing and merrily talking of
trivia. Prayer in the midst of such conversation he
felt sacrilegious. But is not God pleased with the
uplifting of the heart when folks are happy? By such
prayer the laughter before and after is exalted to a
higher plane and presented to the Lord. The social
camaraderie of Jesus exhaled no cold, freezing
dignity but warm gaiety. In complete sympathy He
both wept with those that wept and rejoiced with
those that rejoiced. Laughter did not stop in a home
when He crossed the threshold. Not only was He a
man of sorrows and acquainted with grief but "a
man of joy and acquainted with fellowship," as
someone has said.

HE WAS SUNNY,
SPREADING CHEER TO THE DISCOURAGED

The Lord saw the bright side of things. He told
His disciples He would die, but He added that He
would rise again. When He informed them that in
a little while they would not see Him, He made
sure to promise that a little while later they would
see Him again (John 16:16). When He ate the
Last Supper with them, He promised they would
sup again in the Father's kingdom.

His sunny disposition shed cheer wherever He
went. What joy must have been experienced by
those He healed! The lame man leaps for joy. The
leper who had to cry "unclean" as he lived in a
graveyard outside the city, begging for bread,

unable to go home and embrace his wife or children, is suddenly cleansed! Peter's mother-in-law feels her incapacitating, nagging fever leave her, and out of joyful gratitude rises to minister to those in the house! The blind man who never saw a sunrise nor his mother's face suddenly sees the splendors of nature and the faces of loved ones! The palsied fellow who had to be carried from place to place suddenly feels strength in his body, enabling him to rise and walk! The bent woman who for 18 years couldn't lift herself up straightens at the command of Jesus and glorifies God for joy! The man who was deaf and suffering from a speech impediment suddenly has his ears opened and the string of his tongue loosed! No wonder, though ordered not to tell anyone, he cannot help publicizing it everywhere out of sheer happiness. Unbounded joy made many a cured person disobey Jesus' command to keep it quiet.

Many expressions of Christ command joy positively or negatively. "Be of good cheer," He said to a man He was about to both heal and forgive. He also spoke, "Be of good cheer," to the troubled disciples when they saw Him walking on the water, mistaking Him for a ghost.

Joy-killing fear He ordered banished. How often He said, "Fear not." He dispelled His disciples' fear when He quelled the raging storm on the Sea of Galilee (Matt. 8:26). He warned against anxious worry over material needs in the Sermon on the Mount (Matt. 6:25-34). He calmed Jairus, who had just heard his daughter was dead. "Fear not: believe only, and she shall be made whole"

(Luke 8:50). To His followers He said, "Fear not, little flock; for it is your Father's good pleasure to give you the kingdom" (Luke 12:32).

"Peace to you" or its equivalent was another utterance that promoted joy. To the trembling woman who furtively touched the hem of His garment to be cured of a longstanding illness and who was forced to reveal her identity, He said, "Go in peace, and be whole of thy plague" (Mark 5:34). Someone has said, "Peace is joy resting, whereas joy is peace dancing." Jesus bequeathed peace to His own (John 14:27), that in the midst of tribulation they might have peace (John 16:33). The terrified disciples in the upper room on the day of the Resurrection He greeted with "Peace be unto you" (Luke 24:36).

To the discouraged disciples the Lord twice gave miraculous catches of fish. Downhearted at His impending death they heard Him say, "Let not your heart be troubled" (John 14:1). He promised them a Comforter like unto Himself (John 14:16). He did not have to give the Holy Spirit that particular name, but He did so.

The sinful found the joy of forgiveness through His love. The Samaritan woman was so overjoyed that she forgot her waterpot. Zacchaeus joyfully received Christ into his home.

Those who keep His word will be happy. The beatitudes begin with "Blessed," promising a joyful spirit to those who practice Christlike virtues. Our Lord spread cheer wherever He went, for His desire is that the sunshine of His joy may be found in our lives.

HE WAS SERENE, SELF-POSSESSED,
EVEN SINGING IN THE FACE
OF PERSONAL DIFFICULTY AND DISASTER

He Was Content

Covetousness disrupts contentment. Thoughtful assessment of blessings dispels grumbling and results in thankful praise. A satisfied soul makes a joyful person. Not a single gripe has been recorded among our Lord's words.

The Lord offered thanks many times. He was grateful for daily bread. Before feeding the 5,000 and the 4,000, He lifted up His heart in recognition of His Father's favor in the form of food. Reminder of the Lord's bounties should produce joyful worship.

Christ also thanked His Father for revealing deep spiritual truth to the simple disciples while hiding it from the so-called wise people. He was grateful that one doesn't have to have his B.A. or Ph.D. degree to understand the abc's of spiritual truth.

He also thanked God for answered prayer, "I thank Thee that Thou hast heard Me. And I knew that Thou hearest Me always" (John 11:41, 42).

In addition, the night before He died, the Lord thanked His Father for the bread and wine which pictured His crucified body and shed blood (Matt. 26:26, 27).

Our Lord urged contentment in regard to food, clothing and drink. He practiced what He preached. His joy filled Him with gratitude.

He Was Poised

Thoroughly put to rout by Jesus' words and deeds, the frantic Pharisees, letting rage overthrow reason, held a council to destroy Him. Though they were filled with madness, Jesus was undisturbed. Not indifferent to self-preservation He withdrew but did not flee in panic. His retirement was graced with majestic calm.

He had a wholesome outlook on life. When the Pharisees narrowly objected to healing on the Sabbath, His broader, healthier view realized that they in inconsistency would without hesitation rescue a sheep that had fallen into the pit on the Sabbath. Hence, He proceeded to heal on the Sabbath despite their hypocrisy and anger. He knew He was in the right.

Not the worrying kind, He rested in the Father's care, which enabled Him to live above adverse circumstances. An aura of serenity surrounded Him in all situations.

Doctors tell us that when a thick layer of troubles hangs oppressively over a person preventing him from rising above it into a realm of occasional joy, that person is a candidate for a psychosomatic illness. To avoid such illness we are advised to make our attitude and outlook as cheerful and pleasant as possible. Possession of the joy of Christ has undoubtedly kept many people from psychosomatic breakdown.

Humor involves the recognition of contradiction without loss of inner peace. The Lord not only spotted but spotlighted the inconsistencies of the religious leaders of His day. He described the

Pharisees as those who went around microscopical-
ly examining the eyes of others to discover a
speck therein while at the same time their own
Pharisaical eyes which did the searching had a
piece of lumber protruding from them. He also
described the Pharisees as those who with fringe
of their shawl strained out an insect from their
drink but who then proceed to swallow the
grotesque hulk of a camel, long neck, one hump,
two humps, lumpy knees, hoofs and all. Thus our
Lord used humor. Godly humor springs from
divine joy within and buttresses man in his strug-
gles with the frustrations, tensions, and depressions
of life.

He Sang in the Face of Personal Disaster

The Lord's wish for His followers to have His
same joy is all the more remarkable when the
circumstances under which they were uttered are
recalled. It was on His way to Gethsemane that
He said, "Let not your heart be troubled," and
"I will not leave you comfortless," and "My peace I
leave with you," and "These things have I spoken
unto you, that My joy might remain in you, and
that your joy might be full." In fact, it was in the
garden that He prayed "that they might have My
joy fulfilled in themselves" (John 17:13). In a
few hours Jesus would be arrested, scourged,
mocked, crucified, dead. Yet He was filled with joy.

The night before His death, after instituting
the Lord's Supper, He sang a hymn, probably part
of Psalms 113—118, which was known as the great
Hallel (praise). John the Baptist had been behead-

ed; His relatives thought Him out of His mind; His crowds had dwindled; His disciples would soon forsake Him and flee; Judas was about to betray Him; cruel nails would soon snuff out His life. What was His attitude? Did He complain, find fault, grumble at the way fate had treated Him? No, He sang! So joyful was He in the face of disaster that He sang a psalm in full knowledge that in 24 hours He would be dead after suffering the pangs of the cross. In fact, it was the joy of the Lord which gave Him strength to face the ridicule and pain. His triumphal self-composure on the cross sprang from joy within.

This is why two decades later Paul and Silas, after false accusations, beating, and imprisonment in the inner jail, could sing praises to God at midnight (Acts 16:25). This is why Christians can rejoice when persecuted and treated despitefully. Sorrow and joy are not incompatible. Beneath sorrow can be a substratum of joy which gives strength in the hour of grief. This explains why Paul said he was sorrowful, yet rejoicing. The Christian can be joyful in the midst of miseries, while the non-Christian is often miserable in the midst of his so-called joys.

Where there is the joy of the Lord, singing will be an integral part of life, whether in public worship or private spontaneity. A newspaper writer in a large Canadian city asked why congregational singing is so bad in many churches. He concluded that if you visit some poor little Gospel hall or tabernacle where the economically and socially underprivileged worship with paperbacked songbooks, you will hear some real singing. But if you go to the large stone or brick cathedrals at the city corners where there are towers, spires, stained glass windows, Cadillacs at the curb, striped trousers and mink, you are likely to hear a gentle humming if you listen hard. His explanation was that such people don't practice singing during the week enough, nor do they possess zeal for the Lord. Perhaps they sing so little between Sundays because they have so little devotion to the Lord.

Someone has said, "If you can't sing your theology, there's something wrong with it." We have something to sing about: an omnipotent, loving God above, a Saviour who came to earth to die for us on the cross, the Holy Spirit who lives within, the record of God's message in the Bible, the forgiveness of sins, and a hope of life immortal in a land where our joys shall be forever perfect and our love forever full. A Communistic, atheistic magazine maligned Christianity when it reported the diary entries from a member of the Communist youth organization who infiltrated a group of Soviet Christian youth in 1960. After describing a Christian meeting, it remarked how the service featured hymn-singing, of which the writer commented, "That is their game, you see. They make use of the opportunity to sing as a bait to draw people to religion." The real reason the Christian youth sang was that they had something to sing about, for they were possessed by the joy of Christ.

The Man of Sorrows bequeathed to us a legacy of joy. He came to give the more abundant life, as He proclaimed the glad tidings of the kingdom. One bishop remarked that people will be surprised at last in the presence of Christ to find the Lord so genial. In the parable of the pounds the servant who foolishly hid his talent had a mistaken opinion of his master, calling him "an austere man." But those who used their talents wisely were told to enter into the joy of the Lord.

Finding Christ is like finding buried treasure with which nothing else can compare and for which one sells all else to joyfully possess it. Jesus said, "Rejoice because your names are written in heaven." The Gospel is good news: Christ died and rose. No wonder the women and disciples had great joy when the truth gripped them. Failure to have the joy of the Lord is sin for God's children.

11

Loving Winsomeness

The supreme trait of Christ which we are bidden to emulate is love. This quality Christ Himself enjoined, "A new commandment I give unto you, that ye love one another; as I have loved you, that ye also love one another" (John 13:34). Paul expressed it this way, "Walk in love, as Christ also hath loved us" (Eph. 5:2).

CHRISTLIKENESS CAN BE SUMMED UP IN LOVE

Though love has been left to last, it is the comprehensive quality embracing all others. Love is the principal ingredient in the different characteristics of Christlikeness. In reality, love has been the topic of consideration in every one of the previous chapters, for love is compounded of the elements of nonretaliation, service, self-denial, friendliness, forgiveness, humility, gentleness, and long-suffering. Love is the whole of which these are parts, the hub from which these spokes proceed.

145

Note how closely the characteristics of love in the great love chapter of 1 Corinthians 13 approximate the qualities of Christlikeness described in the preceding pages.

"Love suffereth long"

Love involves the spirit of nonretaliation outlined in the chapter, "So, They Insulted You." Christ, when reviled, suffered long and reviled not again. A soldier, asked how he found Christ, related, "A private in our company got converted. We gave that fellow an awful time. One night when he got down to pray I struck him on the side of the head with my boots. Next morning I found my boots beautifully polished by the side of my bed. That kind of answering back just broke my heart, and I was saved that day."

"And is kind"

The Lord Jesus stooped in kindness to lowly service, as detailed in the chapter, "Service with a capital S." How often He helped as He went about doing good. Augustine became a Christian through the influence of Ambrose. Years afterward, he described the process thus: "I began to love him, not at first as a teacher of the truth, which I despaired of finding in the church, but as a fellow creature who was kind to me."

"Love envieth not"

Christ was never jealous. Can we be happy when another's work prospers and he is praised, or when he is chosen for a position of responsibility?

Or do we burn inside? Genuine love is glad when oil is discovered on a neighbor's property, or when a friend gets a date or becomes engaged, or when a friend is elected chairman (a job we wanted). Love is delighted at the successes of others and grieves at their losses.

"Love vaunteth not itself, is not puffed up"

Christ never bragged, but made Himself a nobody, as is pointed out in the chapter, "Humility of Heaven." Love doesn't advertise itself. Felix Mendelssohn, playing a three-piano arrangement with two other pianists, found that the other two had to concentrate on the score. Though he could easily have played the piece without the music, he positioned some music on the rack and asked a friend to turn the pages for him. Love is not proud.

"Doth not behave itself unseemly"

Christ never acted contrary to good manners. Love isn't disrespectful, nor disdainful of the social conventions, nor does it act disorderly, but decently and in gentleness, as shown in the chapter, "Jesus, the Gentleman."

"Seeketh not her own"

As described in the chapter, "You Aim to Please—But Whom?" Christ pleased not Himself but willingly surrendered residence, radiance, riches, rest, rights, reputation, and life itself. He could have stayed midst the comforts of heaven, but denied self so that we might have heavenly riches, residence, rest, and eternal life. "Greater love hath no man than this that a man lay down his life for his friends."

Therefore followers of Christ should be willing to deny self that others might enjoy spiritual privileges. In fact, we are told that because He laid down His life for us, we should lay down our lives for the brethren (1 John 3:16).

When a church launched an aggressive visitation program, a member had to decide whether to join in the calling or watch a favorite TV program. The thought of Christ's self-denial led him to readily surrender the couple of hours in the warm, soft chair in front of television in favor of the inconvenience of going out into the cold nights to knock on doors with the Gospel.

"Is not easily provoked"

This verse really says that we should not be provoked at all, for the word *easily* was added by some scribe who felt the command too rigorous.

How easily we get irritated. We get irritated at the way the other driver pushes in our lane before we can plug up the gap, at the way someone else squeezes the toothpaste or clears his throat. A wife said of her deacon-husband, who sometimes took charge of prayer meeting, "When I see him on the platform, I think he ought never to come off of it. When I see his behavior at home, I think he never ought to go onto it."

A most common complaint of husbands against wives, and of wives against husbands, is bad disposition. A postman listed the streets on which he delivered and made some notations after certain addresses, such as "Dog barks but doesn't bite," or "Bad-tempered dog." After one address he wrote, "Bad-tempered woman."

Someone wrote,

> "To live above with saints in love,
> That will be glory;
> To live below with saints we know,
> That's another story."

A Christian worker was giving a free dinner at his mission for homeless men. Later, lifting his hat, he found that some of the men, in a prankish spirit, had filled it with bacon rinds and other table scraps. Furious for a moment, he stepped on a chair and delivered a speech in a towering rage. He stormed at the tramps, berating them for their ingratitude. Then suddenly there flashed into his mind the words, "Love is not easily provoked." He lived too near God to fail to realize his error. Then and there he apologized to the men, humbly telling them that he knew he had grieved the Lord. He asked them to forgive him and invited them back for another dinner the following night. The next night nearly 40 men accepted Christ.

A Christian girl, giving a testimony in a crowded service, was interrupted by a man at the back who called out, "That's all right, but how do you behave at home?"

Quick as a flash she responded, "There's my mother, sitting in front of you. Ask her."

The mother rose and said, "She lives at home just as she talks here."

Perhaps the best test of our disposition is at home—where people know us best.

"Thinketh no evil"

Love doesn't keep a record in the mind's ledger of mean deeds committed against it. Love doesn't memorize nor brood over an evil done it, looking forward to paying it back. Instead of carrying around an accumulation of real or imagined wrongs in the mind, love passes a sponge over the entry. Love forgets.

How readily Christ forgave those who trespassed against Him, as related in the chapter, "I'll Forgive, But I Won't Forget." After World War 1 when President Woodrow Wilson urged a greater measure of gentleness toward the defeated nations, French Premier Clemenceau, who then felt more vindictive, objected by saying, "You talk too much like Jesus Christ."

"Rejoiceth not in iniquity, but rejoiceth in the truth"

Love isn't glad on hearing reports of fellow-believers wandering from the Lord. Rather, love rejoices in the truth which recounts the advance of the Lord's work. Christ delighted to hear that the demons were subject to the disciples. The word "rejoiceth" reminds of the chapter, "Joyful Jesus."

"Beareth all things"

The root of the word *bear* is "roof." Love puts the lid on the faults of others, covering a multitude of sins. Love doesn't parade nor discuss the vices of others but stands in the presence of a fault with a finger on its lips. How gracious Christ was with the woman-sinner who in repentance washed His feet with her tears and dried them with her hair.

"Believeth all things, hopeth all things"

Without gullibility nor credulity love takes people at their word. Without suspicion, love puts the best construction on the actions of others, not impugning their motives. Love is optimistic, not pessimistic nor cynical, not slandering nor detracting.

When, after giving someone the benefit of every doubt, we are forced to recognize the ugly fact that this person is a fraud, love does not give up, but hopes even when others have ceased to hope. Just as God now sees sinful men as perfect in Christ, so we should regard other stumbling believers as they will one day be. Christ saw unstable Simon as he would be someday and called his "rock." Love looks through the eyes of hope.

"Endureth all things"

The list of love's characteristics has gone full circle, beginning with "suffering long," and now ending with "enduring all things." Love is surely patient. Someone said, "Isn't it strange that a man can fish all day waiting for a nibble and not get impatient, but when he gets home and dinner isn't ready, he gets mad because he cannot nibble immediately."

Christ was patient under severest provocation. His endurance of sinners' contradiction is reported in the chapter, "In the Hour of Trial."

So, Christlikeness can be summed up in love Someone has said that the great love chapter of the

Bible, 1 Corinthians 13, on which we've been commenting, is really Jesus Christ sitting for His portrait. Notice how easy and natural it is to substitute "Christ" for "love."

> "Christ suffereth long, and is kind;
> Christ envieth not;
> Christ vaunteth not Himself, is not puffed up,
> Christ doth not behave Himself unseemly, seeketh not His own,
> Christ is not easily provoked, thinketh no evil;
> Christ rejoiceth not in iniquity, but rejoiceth in the truth;
> Christ beareth all things, believeth all things, hopeth all things, endureth all things."

A foreign student from a non-Christian culture received a scholarship to a Christian college in America. Students speculated as to which of them would be able to convince this brilliant unbelieving girl into the Christian faith. Later she did become a Christian, but not through the efforts of the campus intellectuals. An insignificant, unimportant, little co-ed won her. When the new convert was asked which argument convinced her of Christianity, the answer came: "She did not use any arguments. She built a bridge of love from her heart to mine, and Christ walked over it."

Christlikeness Relates to Inner Life

Christlikeness is not orthodoxy in the realm of doctrine, as mandatory as sound theology is for the Christian. Christlikeness is love in the area of the disposition.

> May the mind of Christ, my Saviour,
> Live in me from day to day,
> By His love and power controlling
> All I do and say.

We must not lose the sense of importance of this inward life by placing more emphasis on the sins of the outer life. Immorality and drunkenness we may condemn strongly, but we must not regard selfishness, envy, and criticism as insignificant. In reality, sins of the flesh are less satanic than sins of the spirit. Because he has no physical body the devil cannot be guilty of gross physical sins like immorality or alcoholism. But the devil is guilty of the sins which ushered the fall into the universe and ultimately into the world: pride, envy, lying. The sins that led directly to the Crucifixion were not sins of the flesh like adultery or drunkenness, but sins of the spirit: envy, covetousness, lying. How easy it is to condemn others for practices for which we have no scriptural grounds for condemnation, and how easy it is to manifest an unlovely, critical spirit which is clearly forbidden in the New Testament and which runs directly counter to the disposition of Christlikeness which is specifically demanded of us. One woman who didn't believe in reddening her face with makeup had no hesitation about blackening another woman's character.

Christlikeness Revolves Around the Cross

Significantly, most of the qualities of Christ's

example we are bidden to follow center in the cross.

We are not to retaliate because when reviled at the cross He reviled not. Appeal to self-denial mentions taking up the cross. Because He forgave we are also to forgive. The place which made forgiveness possible was the cross. The command to humility is enforced by Christ's condescension, not only to manhood and servanthood, but to the shameful death of the cross.

Patient endurance in persecution is encouraged by the example of Christ who for the joy set before Him endured the cross. The love of Christ is to dominate us because "Christ also hath loved us, and hath given Himself for us an offering and a sacrifice to God" (Eph. 5:2). Later in the same chapter husbands are told to love their wives, "even as Christ also loved the church, and gave Himself for it" (Eph. 5:25).

The night before the cross the Lord stooped to the menial service of washing the disciples' feet.

Primarily the cross made possible reconciliation to God. Secondarily, it illustrates many qualities of Christ which God wants us to cultivate. Thirdly, it provides the dynamic for Christlikeness, for apart from the life of Christ within there can never be the likeness of Christ without.

The Lord's Supper can provide a powerful incentive to Christlikeness. Not only does this ordinance provide a memorial of Christ's crucified body and shed blood for our forgiveness, but it should remind us of His exemplary conduct during passion hours, as illustrated in His love, nonretaliation, forgiving spirit, patient endurance, humility, service, and self-denial. Thus, participation in the Lord's Supper can make us thankful not only for pardon, but can provoke us to copying Christ.

A boy lost in Chicago was taken to the nearby police precinct where an officer knew the major landmarks. He asked the lad if there were any train station, pier, airport, or bus terminal near his home. The boy knew of none. When the boy was asked if he knew of any building, he lit up. "There's a big church with a cross lit day and night. And if you take me to the foot of that cross, I'll know my way home." The cross of Christ not only starts us on the heavenly way and provides a dynamic for the trip, but also gives a vivid picture of the Christlike behavior expected during the heavenward journey.

> By looking to Jesus,
> Like Him thou shalt be;
> Thy friends in thy conduct
> His likeness shall see.

Christlikeness Has Winsome Power

A century ago gold seekers in Montana struck gold in a lonely spot. Because they needed additional supplies and equipment they went to the nearest town after swearing each other to absolute secrecy. Though the vow was faithfully kept, when they started their return to the gold, no less than 300 other gold seekers tagged along. Who had given them away? No one. They had given themselves away, for their beaming faces had betrayed the secret.

Christlikeness is a potent apologetic for the

Christian faith. People would rather see a sermon than hear one. If we belong to Christ, we ought to live like Him. "He that saith he abideth in Him ought himself also so to walk, even as He walked" (1 John 2:6). Wearing a button announcing our Christian faith, or carrying a Bible to advertise our belief, or verbally declaring our allegiance to Christ are legitimate ways of witness. But the indispensible method without which all others are useless and sometimes even harmful is living Christ so people can readily see Him in us. So often what we are speaks so loudly people cannot hear what we say. We must live Him as well as talk Him.

A group of Chinese pastors in the interior of China were once asked what it was about Christ that impressed them most. None mentioned any miracle. One elderly pastor replied, "His washing His disciples' feet." General consensus showed that this moral quality made the biggest impact on them. That a dignified teacher should overstep the lines of class to assume the slave's place was an impressive moral wonder.

How would your life measure up if someone were hired to shadow you for several days to see if you lived in a Christlike way? Some years ago a hospital official watched the lives of professing Christians with whom he came in contact in a large denominational hospital in Atlanta, Ga. "They just don't live what they preach," he concluded, "and if they can't, I can't either."

Someone mentioned the godly life of the pastor of Atlanta's Baptist Tabernacle, Dr. Will H. Houghton, later president of Moody Bible Institute, Chicago. The hospital official decided to see if this man's life was true to his profession. So he hired a plain-clothes detective to follow Dr. Houghton everywhere he went for several days. At the end of the period the detective declared, "He lives it; there's no flaw there."

These words were inescapable evidence. They rang in the man's ears in an hour of great despair when he was about to take his life. With the prayers of his godly wife, these words helped him accept the Saviour. He spent his spare time laboring for the Master in many ways, including the holding of street meetings. His daughter attended Moody Bible Institute, where this story was reported in the student newspaper. The article ends with the daughter's question, "Suppose Dr. Houghton had not lived a sincere, true Christian life—one that would bear watching—where would my dad be today?"

A minister's little boy, after his father had moved to a different parish, rushed in after the first morning of play, "Mother, I've found such a good little girl to play with here. I hope we never move again."

"I'm so happy," said the mother. "What is the little girl's name?"

"Oh," replied the child with sudden seriousness, "I think her name is Jesus."

"What do you mean?" exclaimed the startled mother.

"Well," replied the boy, "she is so lovely and kind that I did not know what other name she could be called but Jesus!"

Too often we are so cross, irritable, and mean that exactly the opposite would have to be said about us. Would that we should live so like Christ that people might wonder if our name was Jesus!

Inspirational Books
for your Enjoyment

Inspirational Books for your Enjoyment

☐ **THE FAMILY THAT MAKES IT** A biblical-approach symposium on the Christian home. Down-to-earth help on keeping a family together in a day when evil forces tear it apart. Textbook **6-2045—$1.75**/Leader's Guide **6-2935—95¢**

☐ **THE FRAGRANCE OF BEAUTY** by Joyce Landorf. Scripturally based study of wrong attitudes that can mar a woman's beauty—and help for correcting them. Textbook **6-2231—$1.25**/Leader's Guide **6-2912 — 95¢**

☐ **ME BE LIKE JESUS?** by Leslie B. Flynn. Discusses the character of the Lord Jesus Christ as examples for a Christian to develop. Textbook **6-2234—$1.75**/Leader's Guide **6-2904—95¢**

☐ **THE SPIRIT WORLD** A study of the occult by McCandlish Phillips, a Christian newsman. Shows the reader he can triumph over the power of Satan by turning to God and His superior forces. Textbook **6-2048—$1.75**/Leader's Guide **6-2900—95¢**

☐ **THE GOOD LIFE** A practical and relevant study of the Epistle of James by Henry Jacobsen, senior editor of Scripture Press All-Bible Adult Sunday School lessons. Textbook **6-2018—$1.75**/Leader's Guide **6-2930—95¢**

☐ **THE STRUGGLE FOR PEACE** by Dr. Henry R. Brandt, Christian psychologist. A fresh and Christian approach to mental health problems. Textbook **6-2023— $1.25**/Leader's Guide **6-2931—95¢**

☐ **BUILDING A CHRISTIAN HOME** by Henry R. Brandt. A practical, biblical, evangelical approach to family living. Textbook **6-2051—$2.00**/Leader's Guide **6-2928—95¢**

**Buy these titles at your local Christian bookstore
or order from Scripture Press.**

Scripture Press Publications, Inc.
Wheaton, Illinois 60187

Please send me the books checked above. I am enclosing $_____ plus 15¢ per book for postage and handling. (Enclose check or money order—no currency or C.O.D.s.)

Name_____

Address_____

City_____ State_____ Zip_____